More Enchanting Friends

Storybook Characters, Toys, and Keepsakes

Dee Hockenberry

Photography by Tom Hockenberry

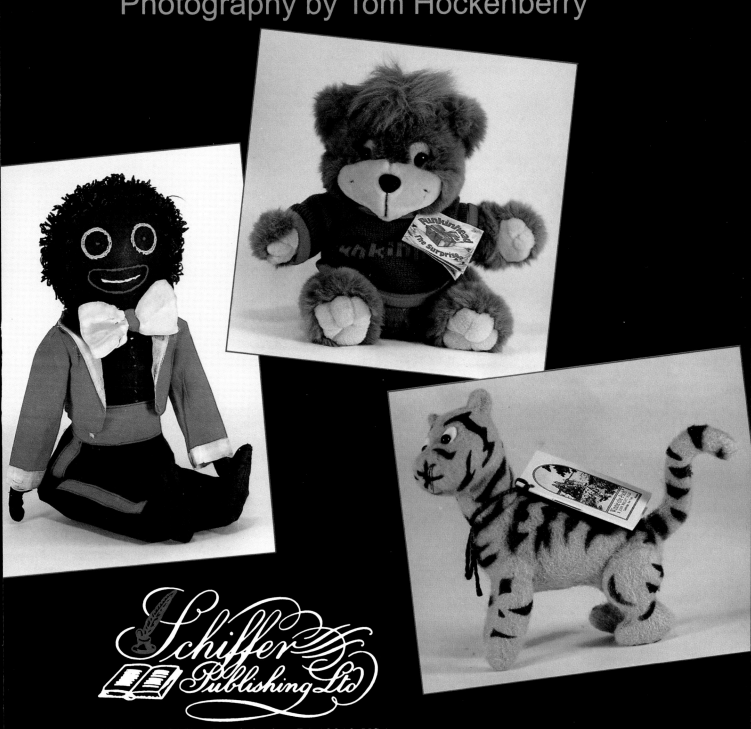

Schiffer Publishing Ltd

4880 Lower Valley Road, Atglen, PA 19310 USA

Dedicated to
Our children Candace and Eric

Remembering
Like the people in this book whose lives revolved around animals, whether
real or imagined, our family has also been enriched by the animals who
shared our home over the years:
The rabbits
Smokey and Flopsy.

The ducks
Henry and Dilly.

The dogs
Butch, Penny, Rufus, Maeve, Hilda Rose, and Josh.

The cats
Foo, Shere Khan, Misty, Pansy, Charles,
Huo Hao, Big Red, Pandora, Tar Baby, Charlie, Francis, Puddy,
Cat Morgan, Pooh,
and the two with us now, Victoria and Albert.

Library of Congress Cataloging-in-Publication Data

Hockenberry, Dee.
    More enchanting friends: storybook characters, toys and
keepsakes/Dee Hockenberry: photography by Tom
Hockenberry.
      p. cm.
    Continuation of: Enchanting friends.
    Includes bibliographical references and index.
    ISBN 0-7643-0513-1 (hardcover)
    1. Character toys--United States--Catalogs.
  I. Hockenberry, Dee. Enchanting friends. II. Title.
NK9509.95.C43H63   1998
688.7'221'075--dc21   97-43826
                      CIP

Copyright © 1998 by Dee Hockenberry

Designed by "Sue"
Typeset in Belwe Bd Bt/Ariel/Times New Roman

ISBN: 0-7643-0513-1
Printed in China
1 2 3 4

The copyrights for all the Disney versions of Winnie the Pooh
are owned by the Walt Disney Company. Copyright holders for all
the A. A. Milne books are Methuen Children's Books Ltd. in London and E. P. Dutton in New York. Curtis Brown, London, owns
the rights to E. H. Shepard sketches. Beatrix Potter books and toys
are copyrighted by Frederic Warne and Co., London. The Raggedy Ann and Alice in Wonderland books are copyrighted by
Macmillan and Co. These companies did not authorize this book
nor furnish or approve of any of the information contained therein.
This book is derived from the author's independent research.

While every effort is made to be accurate, the prices listed are
meant to be a guide and are not to be taken as absolute. Neither the
author or publisher assumes any responsibility to the collector when
either buying or selling.

The Australian Gollies are priced at Australian market value.
Shoppers in the United States should expect to pay double or more.

Published by Schiffer Publishing Ltd.
4880 Lower Valley Road
Atglen, PA 19310
Phone: (610) 593-1777; Fax: (610) 593-2002
Please write for a free catalog.
This book may be purchased from the publisher.
Please include $3.95 for shipping.

Try your bookstore first.

We are interested in hearing from authors
with book ideas on related subjects.

Contents

Acknowledgements and many thanks to:

My publisher and friend, Nancy Schiffer, who makes writing a book almost easy, and my editor, Tina Skinner.

The generous artists, collectors, and companies who sent us photos or allowed us to photograph their collections. They are Judith Armitstead, Celia Baham, Barbara Baldwin, Debby Birli, Maude and John Blackburn of Canterbury Bears, Maria Bluni, Marsha Bohling, Bill Boyd, Candy Brainard, Deborah Canham, Christie's of London, Linda Davis, Gabrielle Designs, Karl Gibbons, Dot Gillett, Nadine Gravatt, John Groff, April Whitcomb Gustafson, Lois Harvey, Donna Hodges, Bonnie Butler Janus, Terri Kovacs, Elsa Malcom, Randy Martin, Victoria Marsden, Pat McCraw, Karen Meer, Becky Mucchetti, Romy Roeder, Beth Savino, Vesna Sheffer, Elena Sodano, Carol Stewart, Lin and John Van Houten, Bonnie and Larry Vaughan, Katie Vogan, Jeanette Warner, Susan Wiley, Lori Woo, David Worland, Richard Wright, Susan and R. John Wright, and Trudy Yelland.

Hugs and kisses to our friends Max Bloch and Sue and Michael Pearson, who drove us around London and West Sussex to our research destinations with good grace, fun, good food, and laughs while on the trails.

To Janie Jones, superb Raggedy artist, who was also so helpful in setting us on the track to Warrington.

I must also acknowledge my indebtedness to Charles Moose for sharing his Seymour Eaton archival collection and to Donna McPherson for her enthusiasm. Donna not only supplied a quantity of Punkinhead material, but made countless efforts to secure data on Seymour Eaton. The responses from Paul MacCallum, principal of Collingwood District Collegiate, Joan Hyslap, archivist, and A. W. Landen, director of Owen Sound Museum in Ontario, were immensely helpful.

Blessings to Mrs. Rutter and John.

Thank you friends, you've all been great.

Introduction

When writing *Enchanting Friends* I was struck by how many threads seem to connect such seemingly diverse subjects. I have discovered even more with this follow-up edition and there are probably others of which I'm not aware.

Theodore Roosevelt always plays a role in any book that relates to bears in any manner. Without the hunting incident in 1902, there would not be a "Teddy Bear." Thus, as a result of the president's activities, we have literary and toy giants named Winnie-the-Pooh, Teddy B and G, Paddington, and Punkinhead. In Florence Upton's book *The Golliwogg in the African Jungle*, Teddy's East African Safari is parodied with Golly adorned in a jungle suit and pith helmet. There is even a drawing of Golly and the Dutch dolls riding on a train's cow catcher in much the same manner as the photograph of T. R. and company that appeared in the press. A little sketch of the president's face is also shown as a dream sequence. It was interesting to learn, as well, that *Alice* was not only a part of Roosevelt's life but also accompanied him on safari. These days it is hard to envision the amount of baggage that was common in the early 1900s. On one hunting trip Roosevelt took, among other things, sixty carefully chosen books including a copy of *Alice's Adventures in Wonderland*.

Golliwogg in the African Jungle, by Florence K. Upton; verses by Bertha Upton; Longman's, Green and Co., London, New York, Bombay & Calcutta, ©1909. Last in a series of thirteen.

Additional associations include Johnny Gruelle's satirical portrayals of Roosevelt when he worked as a political cartoonist. You will find in the Milne/Shepard/Pooh chapter a picture from *The Wind in the Willows,* a version illustrated by Shepard in 1931. This book (an earlier copy of course) was, incidentally, a favorite of the Roosevelt children. A tenuous thread, I admit, but none the less noted. The oddest fact I gathered to add to the Roosevelt Chain concerns a television documentary on his life that I watched one evening. Mention was made that the president was featured in a bizarre version of *The Three Bears*. Unfortunately, no further information was offered other than this brief statement.

The section of London known as Chelsea is beautiful, with tree-lined streets and magnificent houses steeped in history. Many are painted white and they always appear fresh and radiate a brilliance when graced by the sun. Mallard Street, in this area, was the home of A. A. Milne and the birthplace of his son, Christopher Robin. It is, of course, the first home of Pooh and the other animals that became our friends. Florence K. Upton's studio was also in Chelsea—another thread magnified by the fact that a Golliwogg appears on Page 85 of Milne's first Pooh book, *When We Were Very Young*, illustrated by Shepard.

THE ROOSEVELT BEARS
BY PAUL PIPER.

ILLUSTRATED BY R.K.CULVER.

They stepped inside and the man they saw looked them over from head to paw, and with outstretched hand and smiling face he gave them welcome to the place. Said TEDDY-G, when he caught his breath, "I thought this call meant certain death. We armed ourselves with loaded gun when we struck this town of Washington."

THE ROOSEVELT BEARS
(Copyright, 1906, by Seymour Eaton. All rights reserved)

By PAUL PIPER

XXIX. THE BEARS COMPLETE THEIR TOUR OF THE EAST.

When the Bears arrived in Washington
They set out at once to buy a gun.
They bought three guns and pistols ten,
And suits and belts like fighting men.
When dressed complete then off they went
To the house where lives the President.

When they reached the grounds and the entrance gate
No one was near to make them wait.
The news had spread round everywheres
Of this visit planned by the Roosevelt Bears.
A policeman dodged behind a tree
When he got first sight of TEDDY-B.
Detectives wise with eagle eye
Didn't stop to ask the reason why,
But ducked their heads behind a wall
And got under cover one and all.
A doorkeeper in gold and black
Said, "Wait a minute till I come back."
And lawyers bold and statesmen brave
Who make the President behave

Moved out of sight as quick as wink;
To offer help they didn't think;
Though hunting bears wasn't quite their game.
The boys who answer the call of bells
Lost all the breath they use for yells
In crossing lawns in serious fright;
They ran for home with all their might.
And secretaries, three or four,
Got under desks down on the floor
When they saw the Bears at the entrance door.
But one little lad who was playing round
When he saw the Bears he stood his ground
And stepped up bravely to TEDDY-G
And said, "Who is it you want to see?"
Said TEDDY-G in his kindliest way,
"We have traveled East and have come to-day
To see the hunter who doesn't scare
And who isn't afraid of man or bear."
The Bears by the lad were keenly eyed,
And he said, as he beckoned them both inside:
"My dad's in here, but wipe your feet;
I think you're the kind he likes to meet."

They stepped inside and the man they saw
Looked them over from head to paw,
And with outstretched hand and smiling face
He gave them welcome to the place.
Said TEDDY-G, when he caught his breath,
"I thought this call meant certain death.

We armed ourselves with loaded gun
When we struck this town of Washington,
For here 'twas said we'd surely see
The man who chased bears up a tree
And with both eyes shut on darkest night
Could hit a bear and win a fight."
"To stand your ground," said TEDDY-B,
"Is the thing that we Bears like to see;
If fighting's trump or simply fun,
We stand, eyes front, and never run;
But those men of yours who guard your fort
Should be taken West for a little sport
And taught the things you learned out there
When climbing mountains chasing bear."
But he simply laughed at what they said
And joked of stories he had read
In newspapers of things they'd done
On their journey East to Washington.
They talked away for an hour or two
Of hunting trips and friends they knew,
And this country wide and its cities great
From Boston Hub to the Golden Gate.
The Bears were asked to come next day
At an early hour to have a play
On the White House grounds and in children's tent
And to breakfast with the President.

This visit o'er they started out
To see the buildings all about:
The Capitol with its rounded dome,
Where the U. S. Senate makes its home
And congressmen from every State
Gather in halls to deliberate;
The Treasury with its vaults of gold
As much as a dozen trains could hold,
And silver, too, and crisp banknotes
Enough to load a hundred boats;
The Library with its pictured halls
And books stored high within its walls;
The gardens with their trees and flowers,
And a museum where they stayed for hours;
And last of all built straight and high
A shaft that stands against the sky,
Set off with stones which good friends sent
In memory of a President.

TEDDY-G said he would like to see
That famous little cherry tree
And get some cherries, red and sweet,
To take back home to give a treat
To the big raccoon and the mountain goat,
And the old cougar and the young coyote,
To make them square and help them try
To tell the truth and not to lie.
So off they went that day at three
Out in the country the farm to see
Where George's father used to stop
And where the boy learned how to chop.
They found the place as the guide books said
And the cherry stump, but no cherries red;
The stump was there and the hatchet, too,
And neither looking very new.
Said TEDDY-B when these things he saw
And took the hatchet in his paw:
"Of all the shrines of history
Which you and I came East to see
This spot right here I say is trump,
This hatchet and this cherry stump."
TEDDY-G said he would like to try
Little George's ax on a tree near by
To prove to the world that he could do
A trick like that and own up, too,
And chop he did an apple tree
And left a note where all could see,
"This tree was chopped by TEDDY-G."

They breakfasted the following day
With the President and had their play

For an hour before, from early dawn,
With boys and girls upon his lawn.
They asked the President if he
Would come out West their home to see;
Said TEDDY-B: "We'll treat you white
And put you up both day and night
With grizzly bears and panthers wild
And give you sport not quite so mild
As driving congress with its load,
Or riding horseback down the road."
"This strenuous life," said TEDDY-G,
"Is too hard work by half for me;
I'll start back home this very day
And for a month at home I'll stay
And rest my eyes and sleep and eat
And get down again on all four feet."
Said TEDDY-B, "Our journey's through,
There's nothing left to see or do.
We were treated well everywhere we went,
And we have seen the President;
And now for home, that's what I say;
But I mean to journey back this way
To take a boat for London town
To see the king and his golden crown."

The reporters called that afternoon
When they heard the Bears were going so soon
And begged a column at least of news
About their trip and plans and views.

TEDDY-B wrote out his boldest hand
These lines that all can understand:
"To the boys we say be always gay,
And with jolly play fill every day;
Be brave, be true, be square and white,
And don't forget to your friends to write.
And to the girls: We've no advice;
You're every one both sweet and nice.
And to all the people whom we've met,
Please say we leave, with much regret,
For our mountain cave and brook and tree."
Signed "TEDDY-B and TEDDY-G."
As their train pulled out an army band
Played airs well known o'er all the land;
And boys and girls waved their good-bys,
And tears filled many children's eyes.
TEDDY-B called back to the crowd that he
Would come East again each one to see,
And TEDDY-G said he'd do his best
To treat them well if they came out West.

(The End.)

They found the place as the guide books said and the cherry stump, but no cherries red; This stump was there and the hatchet, too, and neither looking very new.

The Roosevelt Bears serial appeared in *The Daily News* on July 21, 1906 prior to publication in book form. The bears meet Teddy Roosevelt; beautifully illustrated by R. K. Culver. (*Photo courtesy of Charles Moose*)

The list of authors and artists who worked at *Punch*, or contributed to this British magazine, is a who's who of celebrities. Among those featured in *this* book are A. A. Milne, E. H. Shepard, Sir John Tenniel, and Florence Upton.

Canada plays a significant role also. Seymour Eaton, creator of the Roosevelt bears, and Ernest Shepard's daughter-in-law were both born there. "Growler," the teddy bear who Shepard used as a model for Pooh, spent his final years in Canada before, alas, being ravaged by a dog. The American black bear who gave her name to Winnie-the-Pooh, began life in White River, Ontario. She was named in honor of her rescuer's home of Winnipeg in Manitoba, (a subject more thoroughly explored in *Enchanting Friends*). Another bear who enjoys popularity is Canada's own "Punkinhead." Lastly, I have Canadian roots myself. My mother was born in Ontario and remained a citizen until her death. I have fond memories of childhood summer vacations spent with my aunt and cousins who still live in that pastoral town.

Winnie and His Friends Poster. The original animals are now housed in the Donnel Center, a branch of the New York City library. Poster is no longer being sold.

Watercolor by E. H. Shepard: 9 x 7 inches; from *The Wind in the Willows*, published by Methuen and Co. Ltd.; 1931; showing Rat and Mole; pencil, ink, and watercolor; not framed; signed "E. H. Shepard." Sold at Christie's, London, December 1996. (*Photo courtesy of Christie's, London*)

I could not end this introduction without mentioning some very nice people who helped me enormously while I was engaged in research. My husband and I, along with our traveling companions, appeared at the Rare Book Department of The Philadelphia Free Library expecting to just walk in. Imagine my chagrin upon discovering that an appointment was necessary. However, all ended well because Karen Lightner, the reference librarian, took pity and not only showed us the original handwritten manuscript by Beatrix Potter, but allowed us to photograph it.

A similar experience occurred in England. Tom and I visit this country as often as possible and have enjoyed the multitude of churches that seem to always be open. Such was not the case with All Saints Parish Church in Daresbury, Cheshire. The sign on the door informed us that the church was open on weekends for guided tours and *this* was midweek. Fortunately the telephone number of a Mrs. Rutter was listed and, as we could spot the red telephone booth close by, we rang her up. The dear lady was ill but said she would try and assist us. Ultimately a kind and generous gentleman named John met us at the church and we had a personal and satisfying day. Certainly we discovered more than would have been possible on our own. In addition to seeing the glorious "Alice" memorial windows, we learned that the baptismal font in the churchyard was used at Lewis Carroll's christening. We were also able to purchase mementos that were housed in a locked case. My thanks are hardly adequate to these three people who so willingly gave of their time and shared these treasures.

The Philadelphia Free Library.

Daresbury Parish Church. The first church was built on this site in 1159 and dedicated to "all saints." The tower is dated 1550 and the rest of the church was rebuilt in 1870–1872.

The Philadelphia Free Library. The rare book department houses a fine collection of Beatrix Potter memorabilia. This includes the autographed manuscript and original watercolors of *The Tailor of Gloucester*.

The Lewis Carroll Memorial Window, dedicated to the author and displaying his famous creatures at the bottom.

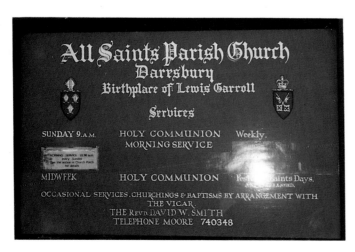

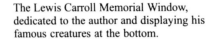

All Saints Parish Church sign.

Baptismal font where Charles Dodgson was christened now resides in the churchyard at All Saints.

Chapter I
Alice and Lewis Carroll's Wonderland

The Adventures of Charles Dodgson

Charles Lutwidge Dodgson describes the place where he was born as a happy spot on an island farm. Indeed, the parsonage at Daresbury in Cheshire, where he was born on January 27, 1832, was set in a sea of corn fields and was a full seven miles from the nearest town of Warrington. Charles, was the eldest of eleven children born to the Reverend Charles Dodgson, who preached at the church in Daresbury and later became an Archdeacon. Unfortunately, only the gate remains of the parsonage and the church is not original, having been rebuilt in the 1870s. With seven sisters and three brothers filling the house and the rather remote location, outside companionship was minimal. The only regular visitors were the Reverend Thomas Bayne, headmaster at Warrington Grammar School, and his son, Vere. Although Vere was three years Charles' senior, the two became lifelong friends.

Charles had a vivid imagination and entertained his family with talent and skill. One of his projects, when very young, was building a train out of a wheelbarrow and conveying his passengers from "station to station" around the garden. He also enjoyed sleight of hand, conjuring, puppeteering, and writing plays. He even wrote a family magazine and one would think that this was the first stirrings of a man called Lewis Carroll.

When Charles was eleven years old, his father was made Rector of Croft in Durham, just over the border from Yorkshire. The rectory was a large brick building with a red-tiled roof and it was to become Charles' home until he was a grown man and moved to Oxford. Education began, however, under the tutelage of his parents. Formal schooling commenced in 1845 at Richmond, a charming country town with cobbled streets and a picturesque ruined castle. While Charles' was matriculating, Mr. Tate, the headmaster, wrote to the Reverend Dodgson of his son's uncommon share of genius. The lad's facility for writing continued and his first story in print appeared in the school's magazine during the first year of his attendance. Unfortunately no copies have survived.

Charles stayed at Richmond for two years and then went on to Rugby, leaving that school in 1849. The following two years were spent at home. During this hiatus he produced another family magazine called *The Rectory Umbrella*. This venture was his most complex to date and, although not yet fully developed, a glimmer of his wit and humor was apparent.

In 1851, just three days before turning nineteen, he came to reside at Christ Church in Oxford. "The House," as Christ Church is always referred to at Oxford, became his home until he died 47 years later. Oxford, at that time, was a medieval collection of university buildings with quaint houses on a small number of streets. Among other undergraduates were Edward Burne-Jones and William Morris (who still has a following for his interesting style of decorating.) Dodgson, for whom mathematics had always been a favorite subject, took first class honors at every examination. He won a scholarship and three years after his entrance was made a "student," the title for one who is a senior and teaches or does research. Other schools refer to this as a "fellow." The scholarship insured his future on the condition that he proceed to Holy Orders and remain unmarried.

Charles was serious and certainly did not shirk his duties yet he found himself a prolific writer on subjects as diverse as parodies for *College Rhymes* and erudite math works. He first used a pen name for a serious poem in 1856 and continued using it as his writings became nonsensical, fearing that academians would frown upon such outpourings. Isn't it strange how life has its little jokes? Very few can name his scholarly works, yet millions have delighted in "Twinkle, Twinkle Little Bat."

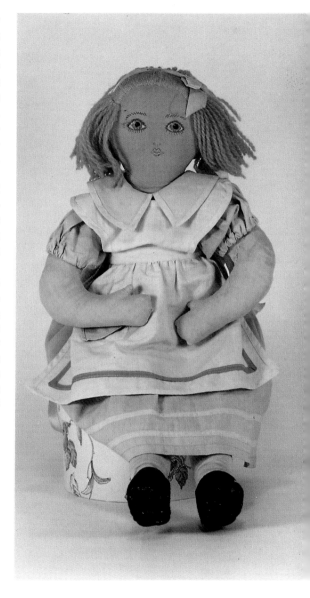

Alice Rag Doll: 19 inches; muslin and cotton with embroidered features and yarn hair; handmade; circa 1930. $350.

Lewis Carroll was hard to identify as Charles Dodgson, the complex man who was shy, reserved, and afflicted with a stammer. He was much more relaxed in the company of children. He visited Tennyson and became fast friends with the poet's children, with whom he carried on a correspondence for many years. Children often visited him in his rooms at Christ Church. He invented stories to amuse them and, because of his proficiency behind a camera, took hundreds of photographs. These included nude studies (a practice that has caused much speculation among his biographers.)

A new dean was called as the head of Christ Church in 1855. Dean Liddell was the father of many children, but it was the three girls—Lorina, Alice, and Edith—whom Charles befriended. They often visited him, accompanied by their governess, and Dodgson in turn became a welcome addition to the Deanery. He taught the girls to play croquet and made a friend of Alice's special pet cat. Many of their activities were later parodied in both *Alice* and *Through the Looking Glass*.

The stories began aloud, very spontaneously, and were meant to amuse the children on their joint excursions. He would often stop and say "That's it until next time," thereby whetting appetites for the following chapter. Alice was the heroine, but Lorina and Edith were there too, as Lory and Eaglet. Dodgson himself was disguised as the Dodo. One day, after an eventful river picnic, Alice proclaimed how much she would love to have the stories written down for her. Charles said he would oblige and even sat up most of the night jotting down all he could remember. When finished he rewrote it all by hand in a little booklet complete with drawings. He had meant it as a Christmas gift, but didn't actually finish it until February of 1863. It was entitled *Alice's Adventures Underground* and was about half as long as the published *Alice's Adventures in Wonderland*.

The vaulted interior of All Saints Church. This photograph shows the altar and the large imposing memorial window.

Author and friend, Henry Kingsley, called on the Liddells one day and happened to pick up the copy. He was so entranced that he urged the family to persuade Dodgson to have it published. Charles was cautious and decided on a second opinion. He lent it to George MacDonald and when read aloud it found as much success as it had at the Deanery. A rewrite involved changes and lengthening and so it wasn't completed until early in 1864. A choice of alternate titles also arose; among them were not only the original but *Alice's Golden Hour* and *Alice in Elfland*. On June 18, 1864, he finally decided on *Alice's Adventures in Wonderland*. After consultation, the artist John Tenniel (who also did cartoons for Punch) was commissioned for the illustrations. Although Alice Liddell had dark hair and bangs, the child Tenniel used as a model was blond. As in A. A. Milne's association with E. H. Shepard, the artist had visions that differed from the author's. Assuredly it made for some clashes, but in both instances the illustrator was correct for we cannot separate our mental images of the artist's works from the written words.

The first stained glass panel in the memorial window.

The fourth panel in the memorial window.

The second panel in the memorial window.

The fifth and last memorial panel.

The third panel in the memorial window

A view of Christ Church College, Oxford, where Charles Dodgson matriculated and taught.

The next step was to find a publisher and Charles eventually entered into an agreement with Macmillan. The firm agreed to present two-thousand copies, but at the authors own expense of £1,319. On July 4, 1865, a full three years after the picnic, Alice received her presentation copy. It has always been assumed that it was Charles who subsequently decided to scrap that first edition, but it was actually Tenniel, who protested strongly against what he felt was a disgraceful printing. Charles agreed and calculated that if the second issue sold out he would break even. Today, rare book collectors would trade large segments of their libraries for a single copy of that very rare first Alice book. Of course, the author did more than break even—*Alice in Wonderland* earned almost unconditional praise. By his death 156,000 copies had been bought by a fascinated public.

Although the sequel, *Through the Looking Glass*, has a date of 1872, it actually came out in time for Christmas of 1871. Before the first issues came off the presses Macmillan already had orders for 7,500, so they printed 9,000 immediately and followed this with an additional 6,000. Three were bound in Morocco for Alice, Ellen Terry's younger sister Florence, and Tennyson. On January 27, 1872, just seven weeks after publication, 15,000 had been sold.

One reason for the popularity of his books is that Charles Dodgson was a trained observer of the most minute details. He understood children, could see life through their eyes, and interpret what they felt with the maturity of an adult. Once he asked a child if she had read the books and her answer thoroughly delighted him for he realized the innocence and straight forwardness of youth. "Oh yes," she said, "I've read both of them, and think that *Through the Looking Glass* is even more stupid than *Alice in Wonderland*."

Charles wrote many other books during his lifetime and they were successful, but it is the two Alice books that are the best-known and best-loved children's books in the English language. The characters are known to more children than any other works of fiction. Charles also saw the books transformed into a West End theater production for Christmas of 1886. It played fifty performances at the Prince of Wales Theatre and then toured major cities. He also invented The Wonderland Postage Stamp Case in 1888 and had it commercially manufactured. The envelope shows Alice holding a pig on the front and a Cheshire cat on the back. When the case is removed from the envelope only the cat's grin remains on the back. It sold for one shilling and who knows what it would fetch now.

Lewis Carroll was known by millions but few realized that the shy, stammering, rather reclusive mathematics teacher, Charles Dodgson, were one and the same. His life at Oxford was simple. He rose early, worked nearly all day, perhaps had a brief walk and a chat with friends and then retired. The worst fate to befall him was the unexplained rift between him and the Liddells. It was devastating to the girls as well. When he and the Liddells met on occasion they were civil but coldly distant. Mrs. Liddell's disdain was so profound that she destroyed the letters he had written to her children and saw to it that neither Charles nor the Alice books were ever mentioned in the Dean's biography.

The Old Sheep Shop in St. Aldates, Oxford, that Carroll and Tenniel used as a model for *Through the Looking Glass*. It is now an Alice memento store and museum.

The Old Sheep Shop Museum sign.

The Mad Hatter's Tea Party, a life-size sculpture on display at a shopping mall in Warrington, Cheshire. The sculpture, by Edwin Russell, was unveiled on May 30, 1984 by their Royal Highnesses the Prince and Princess of Wales.

Alice's Adventures Underground: a facsimile of the 1864 manuscript; paperback ©1965 by Dover Publications Inc. $10-15.

Book: *Alice's Adventures in Oxford*, a Pitkin Pictorial Color Souvenir Guidebook; ©Pitkin Pictorials Ltd., 1980, with details of Lewis Carroll and Alice Liddell.

Charles Dodgson's sitting room at Oxford.

Photograph of Alice Liddell taken by Charles Dodgson; the background painting is by Joseph Mallord William Turner (1775-1851), generally known simply as "Turner."

The Story of Alice in Her Oxford Wonderland, by Christina Björk and Inga-Karin Eriksson; R & S Books; ©1994; hard cover with dust jackets; beautiful photographs and illustrations. $30-40.

When Alice was an adult she made contact with him again and she herself never felt the contempt of her parents. In 1932 on the hundredth anniversary of the author's birth she sailed to New York City for a celebration feted by Columbia University. By this time Lewis Carroll was acknowledged as the greatest children's writer ever. Alice had, however, sold the original handwritten manuscript at Sotheby's auction in 1928. After several additional sales over the years, it was presented on November 12, 1948 to the British Museum in a simple ceremony.

Just prior to Christmas, in 1897, Charles went to stay with his sister at Guilford. On January 6, 1898 he came down with influenza and eight days later died at 2.30 in the afternoon. He is buried under a cross in the shadow of a pine in a lonely cemetery on the Guilford downs. Beneath his own name of Charles Dodgson his tombstone is inscribed:

> *"Lewis Carroll, that the children who pass by may remember their friend, who is now ... in that "Wonderland," which outstrips all our dreams."*

The Writings of Lewis Carroll

The Alice stories made the name Lewis Carroll famous throughout the world. The works, while originally intended for children, appeal to adults as well for they contain a blend of absurdity and logic combined with realism and fantasy. We have become so familiar with the characters and some of their sayings that much of it has become part of our everyday speech. Have you ever, tongue in cheek, emulated the Queen and said "off with her head!" or referred to someone as "mad as a hatter?" While Alice is certainly the most well known, Lewis Carroll saw his name in print on an enormous number of other writings.

Alice's Adventures in Wonderland, 1865
Bruno's Revenge (In Aunt Judy's Magazine), 1867
Phantasmagoria and Other Poems, 1869
Through the Looking Glass and What Alice Found There, 1872
The Hunting of the Snark, 1876
Rhyme? And Reason?, 1883
A Tangled Tale, 1885
Alice's Adventures Underground, 1886
The Nursery Alice 1889,

The Nursery Alice with text adapted to nursery readers; twenty color illustrations Macmillan and Co., London, 1890. $195.

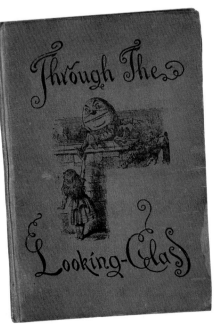

Through the Looking Glass by Lewis Carroll; illustrated by John Tenniel, 1899 edition published by Macmillan and Co., London and New York. $150.

Sylvie and Bruno, 1889
Eight or Nine Wise Words About Letter Writing, 1890
Sylvie and Bruno Concluded, 1893
Three Sunsets and Other Poems, 1898
The Story of Sylvie and Bruno, 1904
Feeding the Mind, 1907
Tour (To Russia) in 1867...1928
The Rectory Umbrella and Misch-Masch, 1932
Collected Verse of Lewis Carroll, 1932
Selection's from Letters to His Child-Friends, 1933

Over the years other publications have appeared by a variety of publishers, writers, and artists. Although the Alice books are parodies themselves, clever people have parodied *them* in extremely witty and imaginative ways:

Alice in Wonderland. Random House, 1955, Illustrated by Marjorie Torrey.
Alice's Adventures in Wonderland and Through the Looking Glass. Phil. Jacobs, 1912. Color illustrations by Elenore Abbot. Black-and-white illustrations by Sir John Tenniel.
Alice's Adventures in Wonderland. Thomas Nelson and Sons. 1908. Illustrated by Harry Roundtree.
Alice's Adventures in Wonderland. Dodge. 1907. Illustrated by Bessie Pease Gutmann.
German edition. Translated by Helene Scheuriesz. Wien und Leipzig 1919. Illustrated by Mela Kohler and Maria Hofrichter.
The Hunting of the Snark and Other Poems. Harper, New York, 1903. Illustrated by Peter Newell.
New Adventures of Alice. Written and illustrated by John Rare. Volland. 1917.

Alice in Wonderland by Lewis Carroll; colorful cover; forty-one black-and-white John Tenniel illustrations; published by McLoughlin Brothers in 1904. $55-65.

Alice in Wonderland panorama book by Raphael Tuck; London, circa 1920; eight panels with sixteen sides: unknown artist. $395.

Alice's Adventures in Wonderland published by W. B. Conkey Company, Chicago; no date, but appears to be about 1915; Janie Jones collection. $25-30.

15

One side of Alice panorama.

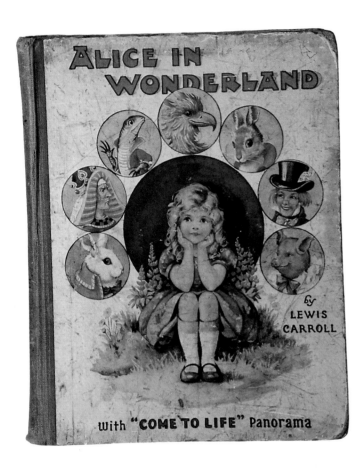

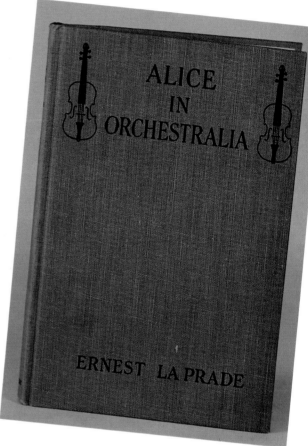

Alice in Orchestralia, a parody of Alice by Ernest La Prade; published by Doubleday, ©1952. $20-25.

Alice Panorama Book. By Lewis Carroll; illustrated by A. L. Bowley; published by Raphael Tuck & Sons Ltd.; 1936; two color plates; sixteen black-and-white illustrations. $195.

Colorful panorama in the center that features all the characters.

Alice in Wonderland, a Juvenile Production Ltd. Edition designed and printed in England. 1930s. $85. *The Original Illustrated Alice in Wonderland.* Tenniel illustrations colored by Martina Selway. Castle Books. 1978. $75. *Through the Looking Glass.* Macmillan, London. 1950s edition. $50.

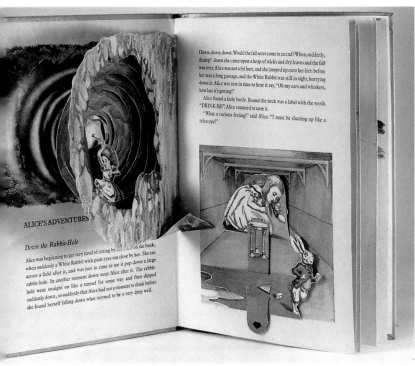

A Macmillan pop-up book, *Alice's adventures in Wonderland*, illustrated by Jenny Thorne after John Tenniel's version. Printed in England with five pop-ups and five moving pictures. 1980. $150.

Cheshire Cat fades as tab is pulled in the Alice pop-up book.

Alice pop-up book showing another moving feature.

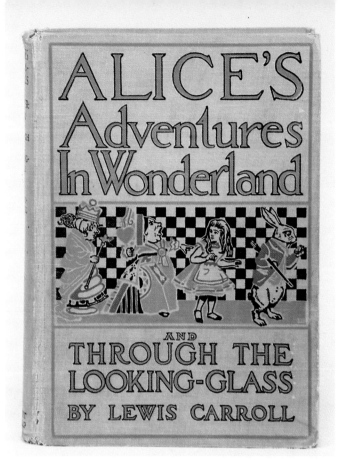

Good Housekeeping Magazine matted cover of March 1923 issue; by artist Jessie Wilcox Smith; showing Alice and many of the characters. $45-50.

Alice's Adventures in Wonderland and *Through the Looking Glass* by Lewis Carroll, a book with photographs and text of a 1930s movie; Viola Savoy as Alice, Herbert Rice as the White Rabbit; published by Gosset & Dunlap. The play was produced by the Nonpareil Feature Film Corporation. $90-100.

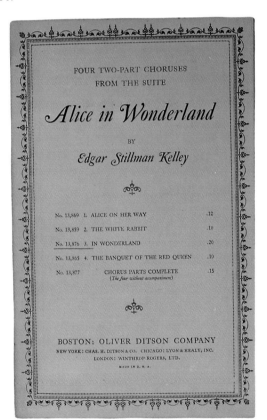

A two-part chorus by Edgar Stillman Kelley; Oliver Ditson Company, Boston, with musical notations for number three in a series of four choruses from the Alice suites; 1925. $45-50.

"Who stole the tarts?" The *Alice* movie book.

AT THE MAD TEA PARTY—ALICE, MARCH HARE, DORMOUSE AND MAD HATTER.

At the Mad Hatter's Tea Party from the *Alice* movie book

THE DUCHESS' KITCHEN.

The Duchess's kitchen from the *Alice* movie.

Songs from *Alice in Wonderland* by Lewis Carroll; illustrations by John Tenniel; music by H. Fraser-Simson; introduction by A. A. Milne; ©1932 Methuen & Co. Ltd.

Playbill from a 1932 production put on by Hunter College students; interesting cover after Tenniel illustrations. $24-30.

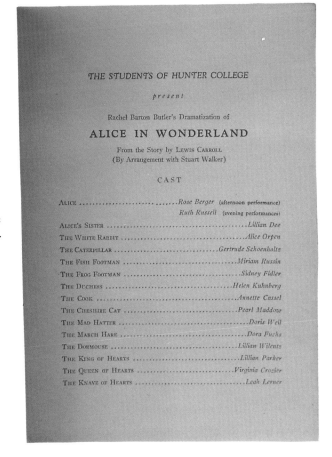

Hunter College cast.

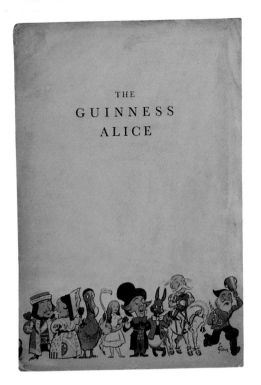

The Guinness Alice, clever parodies offered for entertainment by the Guinness Co., St. James Gate, Dublin, 1933. $155-175.

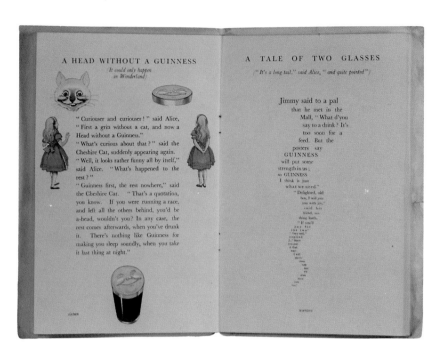

Page from The Guinness Alice, one of the amusing parodies found throughout the booklet.

Souvenir booklet from the Alice in Wonderland Illuminated Garden. The garden opened on September 6, 1933 at Llandudno in Wales with the unveiling of the Alice Memorial. This booklet is filled with photographs of this entertaining amusement park. One enters through a rabbit hole and is fascinated at each step. 1930s. $34-45.

A page from the garden booklet showing some of the scenes.

Alice Versary: The Guinness Birthday Book, celebrating 200 years of business 1759–1959. Another clever parody. $155-175.

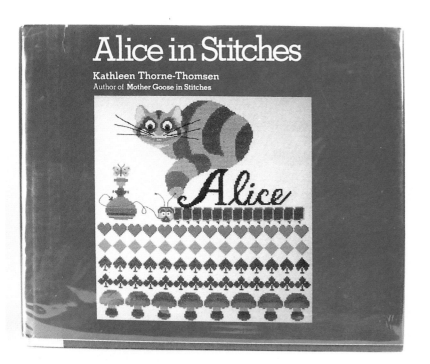

Book: *Alice in Stitches*, a cross-stitch and needlepoint pattern book: includes many characters, from Alice to the March Hare and projects like a stuffed dormouse toy, a child's Alice dress, and the Mad Hatter's tea cloth. By Kathleen Thorne Thomsen; Holt Rinehart and Winston; ©1979. $50-55.

Alice stamp printed in Great Britain in 1979 to commemorate the year of the child. $5-10

Black and white tracing paper with a rendition of the first memorial panel at Daresbury Church; made for children to color. $5-6.

Postcard; available at Alice's Shop in Oxford. $1-2.

ALICE AND THE DUCHESS

Alice and the Duchess postcard; available at Alice's Shop in Oxford. $1-2.

ALICE MEETS THE
CHESHIRE CAT

Alice postcard; available at the Alice Shop in
Oxford. $ 1-2.

Steiff Humpty Dumpty: 13 inch, felt with airbrushed features; shoe-
button eyes, and jointed arms and legs. Steiff made this doll in three
sizes from 1906 to the late 1920s. Steiff was unable to use the name
so they called it "The Man from Mars." Humpty is featured in
Through the Looking Glass. $4,000 and up.

The Mad Hatter: 15 inches and Alice; 12
inches, made by Martha Chase. Painted
oilcloth heads and hands, the rest of the
bodies are cotton and sateen; circa 1920.
(*Photo by Anne Jackson/Richard Wright
collection*)

The Duchess, 13.5 inch, and the Frog
Footman, 13 in: made by Martha Chase.
Painted oilcloth heads and hands; a variety
of cottons and sateens are used for the
bodies and clothing; circa 1920. (*Photo by
Anne Jackson/Richard Wright collection*)

Tweedledee and Dum: 13 inches; all felt with wire armatures; British; handmade; circa 1950. $275 pair.

Alice: 10.5 inches; cloth doll with printed features; commercially made; 1940s; $95. (*Becky Mucchetti collection*)

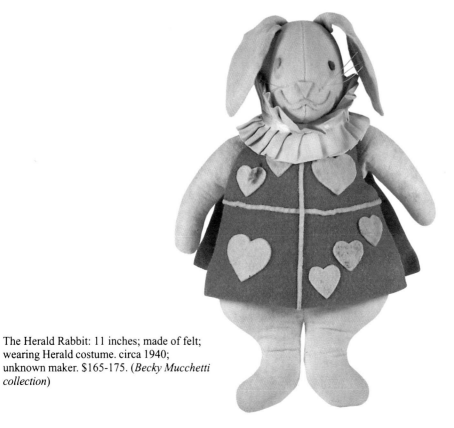

The Herald Rabbit: 11 inches; made of felt; wearing Herald costume. circa 1940; unknown maker. $165-175. (*Becky Mucchetti collection*)

Alice and friend: 20 inches; muslin with painted face; fine yarn hair; velvet dress; satin and lace apron; white stockings and shoes; felt rabbit; made by Rebecca Iverson in 1983. $500. (*Becky Mucchetti collection*)

The White Rabbit: 15 inches; muslin with finely detailed clothes; made by Rebecca Iverson; ©1984. $500. (*Photo courtesy of Becky Mucchetti*)

The Mad Hatter: 13 inches; felt and cotton; yarn hair; amusing facial treatment; British; handmade; circa 1950. $150.

Alice doll: 8.5 inches (plus stand). Made by the late British doll designer Ann Parker; 1980s; permanently mounted; $350-plus. (*John Groff collection*)

The Mad Hatter: 15 inches; muslin and finely detailed clothes; made by Rebecca Iverson; ©1984. $500. (*Photo courtesy of Becky Mucchetti*)

Alice: 15 inches; muslin with fine cotton yarn hair and beautifully made dress and apron; made by Rebecca Iverson; ©1985. $500. (*Photo courtesy of Becky Mucchetti*)

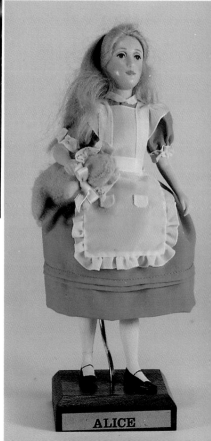

ALICE

Alice caterpillar figure: 7 inches; ©1990 by Gladys Boalt; finely hand-painted on muslin; considered a tree ornament. $45-50.

Alice with Flamingo: 6 inches; ©1980; by Gladys Boalt; handmade of muslin and hand painted; cotton clothes. $45-50.

The Cheshire Cat: 5 inches; painted muslin; by Gladys Boalt; circa 1980. $45-50.

The Mad Hatter ornament: 7 inches including hat; cotton and felt with hand-painted face; meticulous attention to detail by artist Gladys Boalt; cord for hanging; l990s. $45-50.

Duchess with baby: 7 inches; ©1990 by Gladys Boalt; detailed muslin, cotton, and lace; hand made and painted. $50-55.

Humpty Dumpty figure: 4 inches; ©1980 by Gladys Boalt; hand-painted; muslin, cotton, and felt clothes. $40-45.

American character "Sweet Sue:" 14.25 inches; this Alice doll is made of hard plastic and has open and close eyes; replaced socks; circa 1950. $245.

Madame Alexander Alice: 13 inches; vinyl head; plastic body; all original; mint in box. $115.

American character "Sweet Sue" Alice: 17 inches; hard plastic; saran wig; 1952; unmarked. $250. (*Becky Mucchetti collection*)

Steiff Alice and her friends: includes the White Rabbit, the Cheshire Cat, and a mouse; doll by Suzanne Gibson; 1986. $350-400.

The Duchess: 7 inches; resin face, head and body; exquisitely made by doll artist Hintmark; 1995. $ 175-195.

Copperplate engraving: 3 x 2 inches including frame; open edition of 1982; John Anthony Miller, artist and engraver; burnt sienna ink on sixteen-gauge copperplate; entitled "Alice's Fantasy." $300. (*Beth Savino collection*)

Alice: resin molded by artist Vesna Sheffer. 1996. $25. (*Photo courtesy of Vesna Sheffer*)

Limited edition print: 6 x 9 inches; from *Alice's Adventures in Wonderland*; the "Drink Me" passage from Chapter One; numbered print from the original wood engravings on acid-free paper, loosely inserted in an acid-free slip case; title and quotation on the front; only 250 copies made; ©1988 Macmillan. $350.

Cover of "Alice Drink Me" print.

Prospectus for Alice print: ©1987 Macmillan; 1,000 copies printed at the Rocket Press.

Alice print: 8 x 10 inches matted; John Tenniel sketch of Alice after she "grew." Antique print matted and hand colored. $34.

The Red Queen print: 8 x 10 inches matted; John Tenniel sketch (antique) that has been matted and hand colored. $35.

Alice and the Knight print: 8 x 10 inches matted; antique Tenniel sketch that has been matted and hand colored. $35.

Alice's kitten print: 8 x 10 inches matted); antique Tenniel sketch that has been matted and hand colored. $35.

Alice and Tweedledum print: 8 x 10 inches matted; antique Tenniel sketch that as been matted and hand colored. $35.

Alice print: 8 x 10 inches matted; antique Tenniel sketch that has been matted and hand colored. $35.

The White Queen print: 8 x 10 inches matted; antique Tenniel print that has been matted and hand colored. $35.

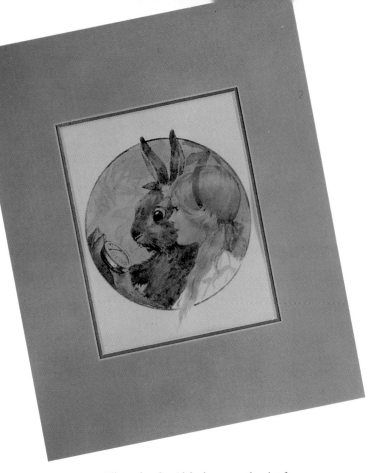

Alice print: 8 x 10 inches matted; print from
book illustrated by Margaret Tarrant; 1926;
Alice looking at the funny watch. $50.

Alice print: 8 x 10 inches matted; print from
book illustrated by Margaret Tarrant.

Alice print: 8 x 10 inches matted; print from
book illustrated by Margaret Tarrant.

Alice print: 8 x 10 inches matted; print from
book illustrated by Margaret Tarrant; 1926;
the Cheshire Cat looking at the King. $50.

Alice in Puzzleland Game: Object is to manipulate the metal balls along the path and finally into the Mad Hatter's Tea Party; British; made by R. Journet & Co.; circa 1950. $110-125.

Hand-held game: 2 inches; British; showing the Red Queen; object is to get the three balls in the holes; circa 1920. $95.

Alice Magic Lantern slides: 4 x 4 inches; boxed set of twenty-four beautifully colored Tenniel illustrations; produced in England pre-1900; must be seen through light. $550-575.

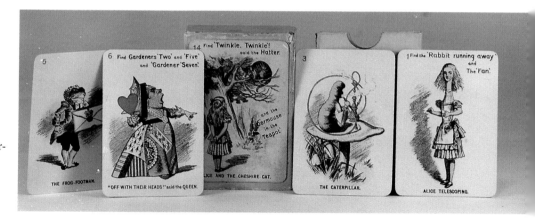

Alice in Wonderland playing cards: Wonderful graphics; manufactured by Thomas De La Rue & Co. Ltd., England; circa 1900. $225-250.

Alice in Wonderland Game: Milton Bradley ©1933; with Tenniel style drawings and photographs from the motion picture; produced by permission of Paramount Productions Inc.; board and cover only. $125-140.

Gameboard for the Alice game.

Alice in Wonderland board game: Parker Brothers Inc.; circa 1940. $145-150.

Panoramic paper roll. 4 inches long; paper roll on wooden reel; two colored panels to give movement effect; used in a Jecktor machine; Dandy Films 1933; The Movie Jecktor Co., New York. $135-145.

Alice in Wonderland chess set: resin with stone castings; hand glazed; made by Adult Leisure Products Corp.; ©1966. $400. (*Beth Savino collection*)

Alice and the White Knight tile; 6 inches square; made in England; circa 1935. $85-90.

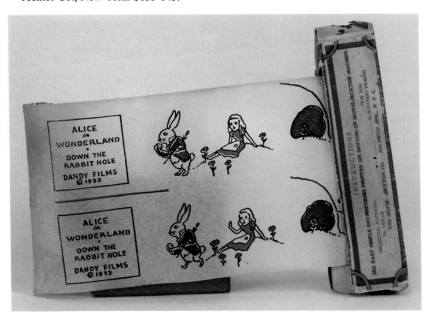

The Walrus and the Carpenter tile: 6 inches square. White Rabbit tile: 6 inches square. Made in England, circa 1935. Purchased with remains of cement on reverse; possibly removed from a fireplace surround. $85-90 each.

Biscuit tin money box in the shape of a cottage; showing the Mad Hatter, the March Hare, and the Dormouse; circa 1935; made for MacFarlane Lang & Co. Biscuit and Cakes, Glasgow & London. $155-165.

Alice in Wonderland clock: made in England; battery operated; 1990s. $100

Tetley Tea tin: 4.25 inches; showing characters from Alice in Wonderland on all four sides; originally held fifty-four tea bags; circa 1950. $95-100.

The Mad Hatter's Tea Party: unusual and creative painted wooden ensemble, tray represents a walled garden with painted flowers and carved trees and gate; free-standing parts include two pine trees, a table and four chairs, a teapot, cup and saucer, and four exquisitely detailed and fully articulated figures of the Mad Hatter, the March Hare, Squirrel, and Alice; circa 1930. $375-400.

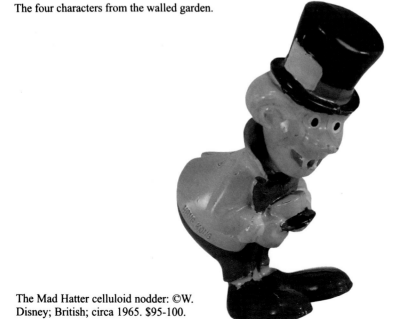

The four characters from the walled garden.

Griffin: 6.75 inches; wood cutout; jointed; part of "Alice" set; circa 1930. $45-50.

Humpty Dumpty: 4 inches; wood cutout; jointed; part of "Alice" set; British; circa 1930. $45-50.

The Mad Hatter celluloid nodder: ©W. Disney; British; circa 1965. $95-100.

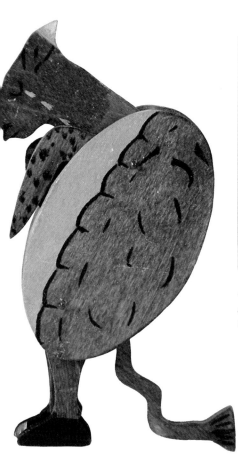

The Red and White Queens: 3.5 inches and 4.5 inches; from *Alice Through the Looking Glass;* circa 1930. $45-50 each.

The Mock Turtle: 4 inches; British; cutout; part of "Alice" set; circa 1930. $45-50.

The Walrus, 3 inches, and the Carpenter, 4 inches: part of "Alice" set; circa 1930. $45-50.

The Mad Hatter, 5 inches, and the Duchess, 4.5 inches: part of British "Alice" set; circa 1930. $45-50 each.

Alice, 3 inches, and the Red Queen, 3.5 inches: part of set; circa 1930. $45-50.

Birds, duck, croquet mallet, and balls: 1-2 inches; from the Alice set; circa 1930. $7-10 each.

The Cook: 4 inches; from the Alice set, circa 1930. $45-50.

The White Rabbit, 4.5 inches, and the March Hare, 5 inches: from the Alice set, circa 1930. $45-50.

Birds, 1.5 inches, and lobster, 1.25 inches: from the Alice set; circa 1930. $10-12 each.

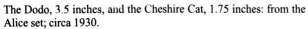

The Dodo, 3.5 inches, and the Cheshire Cat, 1.75 inches: from the Alice set; circa 1930.

Calendar: 3 inches; plastic with paper monthly inserts; the White Rabbit from Alice's Adventures; British product although foreign made; circa 1950. $95-100.

Cheshire Cat: 2.75 inches; painted plaster; sold at Disney World in the 1980s; ©W. Disney. $15-20.

Alice in Wonderland tea set comprising a teapot, sugar basin, cream pitcher, three plates, and three cups and saucers; no marks but suggests German origins; not after Tenniel; luster ware; circa 1890. $375-400.

The cup atop the Sugar Basin showing unusual rendition of the Mad Hatter's Tea Party. Writing around the edge of picture reads "There Alice saw beneath a tree their elbows on a table set/for tea the March Hare and the Hatter, between them the/Dormouse in his usual doze awoke when they poured/on his nose and told a tale that didn't matter."

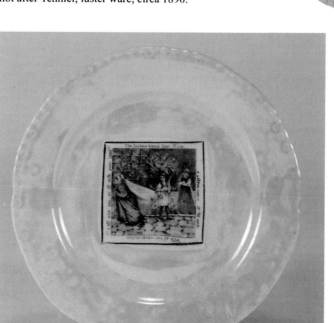

One of the plates from Alice Tea set; showing Alice, the Queen, and the Duchess; printing around the edge reads "The Duchess teased Dear Alice/The Queen came by and said/with all her usual malice/It's off with *you* or your head!"

37

Alice Mustard Pot: 4 inches; hand-painted bisque showing the Duchess and Baby, Alice, Cook, and Cheshire Cat; marked "RD 446134;" circa 1900. $375-400.

Alice egg: 3 inches; hand-painted bisque; the same artist and scene as on the mustard pot; impressed "968;" circa 1900. $250-300.

Tweedledee and Tweedledum pitcher: 3 inches; part of a series with Alice characters as the theme; German; circa 1900. $225-250.

Plate: 5 inches; German; showing Alice, the Flamingo and the Duchess; circa 1900. $140.

China egg: 4 inches; showing Alice and Tweedledee and Tweedledum; impressed "969" on bottom; circa 1900. $425-450.

Plate: 9 inches; the Walrus, and the Carpenter; German; circa 1900. $225.

Alice china plate with scene of Mad Hatter's tea party; circa 1920; made expressly for Harrod's Department Store. $250-260.

Plate: 5 inches; Alice with Tweedledee and Tweedledum; German; circa 1900. $140.

Alice bowl: 6.5 inches in diameter; British ironstone pottery showing the Walrus and the Carpenter with text around the edge; made by Johnson Bros.; circa 1950. $145-150.

China plate: 8 inches; Alice at the Mad Hatter's Tea Party; produced by Johnson Bros.; England; circa 1950. $38-40. Smaller china plate: 5 inches; Alice with fish footman and the White Queen; part of the same set as the larger plate. $28-30.

China Bowl: 6.5 inches English; made by Johnson Bros.; features Alice with Tweedledee and Tweedledum; circa 1950. $35-40.

Royal Doulton pitcher: 7 inches; the Cook and the Cheshire Cat; ©1989. $250-plus.

Alice in Wonderland tea set: plastic; forty pieces; made by Reliable Toy Co. Ltd. of Toronto; circa 1955. Original price tag of $13.95 Canadian; plastic cover could not be removed for photograph. $50-55. (*Donna McPherson collection*)

Silk mat with fringe: 7 inches square. Hand painted in England showing Alice, the Knave of Hearts, the Flamingo croquet mallet, and the Cheshire Cat's face in the sky; beautifully rendered; possibly one of a kind; circa 1900. $195-200.

Table mat: the Lobster Quadrille.

Table mat: The Mock Turtle's Story.

Six table mats: 7 inches in diameter; white cotton with lace borders; scenes from Alice hand-sketched in ink; late Victorian; initialed "A. B. M." Quotes: "Who are you? Said the Caterpillar." $225-250 set.

"You are old said the youth;" one of three mats featuring this character.

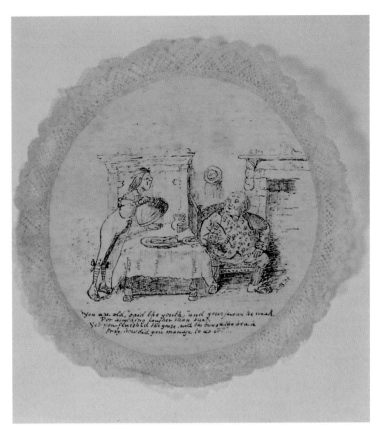

"You are old said the youth;" one of three mats featuring the youth.

"You are old said the youth;" one of three mats featuring the youth.

Alice cotton bags with *Alice in Wonderland* fabric that has been cut and sewn into travel shoe bags; printed in England; circa 1960. $15 each.

Alice tea cozy; British; scene from the Mad Hatter's Tea Party; 1996. $15.

Alice tea towel: sepia colored Tenniel illustrations on a white background; linen; British; 1996. $10.

Cheshire Cat T-shirt: adult size; cat glows in the dark; 1990s. $35.

Back of Cheshire Cat T-shirt: the glow-in-the-dark words "We're all mad here, I'm mad, you're mad."

Alice spoons: silver plate, enamel handles; made in England; 1990s. $15-18 each.

China plate: 6 inches; annual plate for sale at All Saint's Church in Daresbury, Cheshire; features characters from Alice in Wonderland; 1995. $10-15.

Enamel box: 1 inch; made by Halycon Days; England; 1995.

China plate: 6 inches; annual plate produced for sale to raise funds for The All Saint's Church in Daresbury; transfer design showing Alice, Tweedledee, and Tweedledum with the church in the background; 1996. $10-15.

Figurine advertisement: a six-piece set ranging in size from 3-4 inches; offered by "Lawleys by Post" in 1996 for £150 (approx. $250).

The Cheshire Cat, copyright W. Disney, a Disney store display item.

The Mad Hatter, copyright W. Disney, a Disney store display item.

Chapter II
The Magic of Raggedy Ann

Johnny Gruelle's Legacy

Reproduction of the original patent design for Raggedy Ann.

Raggedy Ann prototype: drawing by Johnny Gruelle for the Ann patent; Sept. 7, 1915. This was reproduced for a poster and colored by Worth Gruelle.

Johnny Gruelle left behind a monumental legacy in the world of children's literature and playthings. All his life he appeared to have marched to the beat of a different drummer and that, perhaps, is the criteria of a true artist. He was born in December of 1880 in Arcola, Illinois, but was able to call many other cities "home" as he pursued his chosen profession. Johnny began his career as a cartoonist, working on several different newspapers while gaining a reputation as a major satirist and winning awards along the way.

In 1916, when his beloved daughter, Marcella, died from a contaminated vaccination needle, he immortalized her with a series of books starring the child's rag doll. *Raggedy Ann Stories* was first published by the P. F. Volland company in 1918. A multitude of other titles appeared in the following decades; some published posthumously. Additional copyright holders include M. A. Donahue, J. Gruelle Co., McLaughlin, Myrtle Gruelle Co., Bobbs-Merril, and McMillan. The majority of these books were self illustrated, but because so many manuscripts were found after his death, in 1938, the task of illustrating these works was admirably filled by his son, Worth, and brother Justin. Since 1940, other editions in various formats have appeared with different artists (as well as new stories) bearing the Raggedy Ann name.

After reading and delighting in the adventures of this appealing doll it seemed as if every child in America clamored for a toy just like the one in the book. John and his family set to work sewing the replica until the job grew to Herculean proportions. The reins were then yielded to Volland, who subsequently produced both Andy and Beloved Belindy. Volland dolls have an almost folk-art charm and are eagerly sought by collectors everywhere. The next firm to hold the license was the Exposition Toy and Doll Company, whose tenure was a scant six months. In 1938, Georgene Novelties produced them and over the following twenty-five years made changes that should be noted by studying photographs as well as handling the dolls themselves. The Knickerbocker Toy Company was the next legal representative, eventually turning the manufacturing rights over to a division called Applause. When Applause merged with Wallace-Berrie, some of the production became the property of Hasbro.

Several companies fashioned the popular dolls by making enough alterations to circumvent licensing laws. Among those are Little Eva and The American Toy and Novelty Manufacturing Co. In 1935, Mollye Goldman of Mollye's Outfitters simply pirated the idea and did not desist until a lengthy court battle forced her to abandon production a full three years later.

The number of related mementos and playthings began almost as early as the doll's inception and continues with no signs of abating. They are fabricated worldwide with enough diversity to satisfy both children and the more sophisticated collectors. John's grandson, Kim, is the proud proprietor of a store in North Carolina called "The Last Great Company." It houses shelf after shelf of Raggedy products and is a fitting monument to John Gruelle and the Raggedy Enterprise. There is a store devoted entirely to the charming creature within twenty-five miles of my home. It's located in Spencerport, New York, and named "The Raggedy Schoolhouse."

Every summer a celebration of Johnny Gruelle's life and works is held in Arcola, Illinois, the city of his birth. Devotees attend from far and wide to share and purchase the many items available. A number of talented doll artists feature their own special renditions and they have developed a dedicated following.

Raggedy Ann and her playmates are recognized and adored by children and adults from one end of the globe to the other. It is the rare child indeed who has not at one time held Raggedy close to her heart and heard the beat of the doll's heart that encircles the most poignant of words: "I love you."

Raggedy Ann and Andy Books

Although the majority of the Raggedy series were written and illustrated by Johnny Gruelle, a number of manuscripts were found following his death in 1938. These were published and illustrated by his son, Worth, or his brother, Justin. The books that were issued by Volland were beautifully presented in boxes and with dust jackets. It is difficult to find them in this original condition, so they are very valuable. Expect to pay accordingly for any first edition, as well, particularly for those published before 1935.

Raggedy Ann Stories, 1918
Raggedy Andy Stories, 1920
The Camel with the Wrinkled Knees, 1924
Raggedy Ann's Wishing Pebble, 1925
Raggedy Ann and Andy Alphabet Numbers, 1925
Raggedy Ann's Alphabet Book, 1925
Beloved Belindy, 1926
Raggedy Ann and the Paper Dragon, 1926
Raggedy Ann's Magical Wishes, 1928
Marcella, 1929
Raggedy Ann in the Deep, Deep Woods, 1930
Raggedy Ann in Cookieland, 1931
Raggedy Ann's Lucky Pennies, 1932
Raggedy Ann and the Left Handed Safety Pin, 1935
Raggedy Ann in the Magic Book, 1939
Raggedy Ann and the Golden Butterfly, 1940
Raggedy Ann in the Garden, 1940
Raggedy Ann Helps Grandpa Hoppergrass, 1940
Raggedy Ann Goes Sailing, 1941
Raggedy Ann and the Nice Fat Policeman, 1942
Raggedy Ann and Betsy Bonnet String, 1943
Raggedy Ann and the Laughing Brook, 1943
Raggedy Ann in the Snow White Castle, 1946
Raggedy Ann at the End of the Rainbow, 1946
Raggedy Ann and Andy's Friendly Fairies, 1960
Raggedy Ann and the Hobby Horse, 1961
Raggedy Ann and the Happy Meadow, 1961
Raggedy Ann and the Wonderful Witch, 1961
Raggedy Ann and the Golden Ring, 1961

Raggedy Andy prototype: drawing by Johnny Gruelle for the Andy patent. Patented August 11, 1917.

The dates given are for the first time the books appeared in print and most have been reprinted by either the original publisher or later copyright holders. Some of the later titles are based on stories attributed to him. There are many other volumes that may be found by a diversity of writers, artists, and publishers, all with the Raggedy theme.

Original advertisement that appeared in the *Boston Transcript* in 1919 advertising the *Raggedy Ann* book by Volland; shown with a photo of a child reading the book and holding the doll; photo is of the same period. (*Becky Mucchetti collection*)

Raggedy Ann: 15 inches; beautiful prototype rendition by artist Janie Jones; 1995. $80.

Raggedy Andy: 15 inches; superb rendition of the Andy prototype by artist Janie Jones.

Raggedy Ann's Sunny Songs: by Johnny Gruelle and Will Woodin; Miller Music Inc. publishers; ©1930. $195-225.

Raggedy Ann and Andy book: with animated illustrations by Julian Wehr; ©1944 Johnny Gruelle Company; The Saalfield Publishing Co.; by pulling the tabs part of the picture moves; with dust jacket. $180-225.

Raggedy Ann: 16 inches; sweet-faced doll with shy expression; painted face; made by Volland; wooden heart; replaced apron; marked on back; circa 1921. $1,000-1,100.

Page showing pull-tab animation.

Volland Ann: 15 inches; all original; mend on neck; wooden heart; circa 1920. $1,250.

Raggedy Ann: 16 inches; made by Volland; one of the first produced; stamped on back; wooden heart in body; original clothes; replaced hair; played with condition. $600-plus.

Showing date stamp on back of Ann.

Raggedy Ann: 16.5 inches; made by Volland; printed face (this is considered the second printed face model); wooden heart; un-marked; circa 1918. $2,000. (*Becky Mucchetti collection*)

Raggedy Ann: 16.5 inches; made by Volland; hand-drawn face; longer dress; wooden heart; marked on back; circa 1920. $1,000-1,100. (*Becky Mucchetti collection*)

Raggedy Ann, 6.5 inches, made by Volland, unusually large white eye circles, painted face, missing one hand, wooden heart, marked on chest, circa 1919. $850-900 (*Becky Mucchetti Collection*)

Raggedy Ann: 17 inches; made by Volland; printed face; all original; note the "pencil stripe" legs; wooden heart; marked on back; circa 1920. $950. (*Becky Mucchetti collection*)

Mystery Ann: 20 inches; stencil-printed face; shoe-button eyes; wooden heart; vintage fabric; appears to be commercially made; 1920s-1930s. $500-plus. (*Becky Mucchetti collection*)

Ann: 7 inches; handmade; 1920s; $250. (*Becky Mucchetti collection*)

Raggedy Ann: 18 inches; sweet-faced Volland; circa 1920; wooden heart can be felt in her chest; replaced hair, apron, and pantaloons (all with old materials). $1,500.

Handmade Ann and Andy: 23 inches and 24 inches; painted features; glass button eyes; looped wool hair; frail cotton clothes; circa 1920. $500 pair. (*Becky Mucchetti collection*)

Raggedy Andy: 16 inches; made by Volland; circa 1920; all original including the clothes; damage to thumbs. $600-plus.

Raggedy Andy: 16 inches; Volland; painted face; all original except for tie; circa 1925. $1,000. (*Becky Mucchetti collection*)

Raggedy Andy: 16.5 inches; Volland; painted face; large thumbs; elbow seams; circa 1919. $950-plus. (*Becky Mucchetti collection*)

Volland Andy: single-lash style; circa 1928; original clothes. $2,500. (*Candy Brainard collection*)

Beloved Belindy: 15 inches; all original; missing collar; painted face; wooden heart; made by P. F. Volland Co.; 1926. $3,000. (*Becky Mucchetti collection*)

Cleety: 11.5 inches; character from Raggedy book; handmade; appears to be from the 1920s. $250. (*Becky Mucchetti collection*)

Little Eva Ann and Andy; 24 inches; cotton with yarn hair and shoe-button eyes surrounded by ten embroidered eye lashes; leather shoes; made by Little Eva Washable Toys; circa 1925. $1,300-1,800 pair. (*Judith Armitstead collection*)

53

Mollye's Raggedy Ann: 17 inches; all original; signed on chest; circa 1935. $1,800.

Exposition Doll and Toy Co. made this Ann for less than one year, from late 1934 until the middle of 1935; the tag is on the bottom of the dress hem; complete and original; rare. $4,500-plus. (*Candy Brainard collection*)

Mollye's Ann: 18 inches; all original; retains hang tag; circa 1935. $2,000.

Handmade Ann: 20 inches Wool hair; painted features; circa 1930. $75. (*Becky Mucchetti collection*)

Percy Policeman: 15 inches; made by Volland; circa 1930; missing hat; rare. $2,500-plus. (*Candy Brainard collection*)

Georgene Ann, and Andy: 19 inches; all original; tags sewn into side seams; circa 1940. $1,650-plus for pair.

Mollye's Raggedy Andy: 17 inches; all original; missing hat; signed on chest; circa 1935.

Raggedy Andy: 18 inches; made by Mollye's Doll Outfitters; retains original wrist tag. $1,800-plus. (*Bonnie and Larry Vaughan collection*)

Wrist tag found on Mollye's Andy has "Raggedy Andy/Trade Mark" on front, "Mollye's/Trade Mark" on reverse.

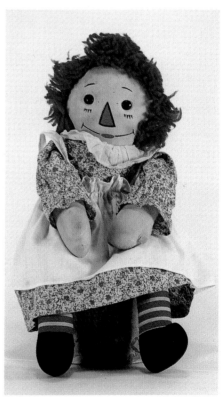

Georgene Ann: 18 inches; circa 1940. Note the unusual print color used in the dress. $595.

Georgene Awake/Asleep Ann: 13 inches; black-outlined noses; all original; label on side of body; circa 1940. $450-plus.

Asleep side of Georgene Ann.

Georgene Ann: 15 inches; tagged; 1947. Note the unusual animal printed dress. $400. (*Candy Brainard collection*)

Georgene Ann and Andy: 19 inches; mint-in-box with all labels intact; circa 1953. $1,400 pair. (*Becky Mucchetti collection*)

Beloved Belindy: 18 inches; all original; forward-facing feet; original advertisement; made by Georgene; circa 1950. $1,500-plus. (*Becky Mucchetti collection*)

Beloved Belindy: 18 inches; all original; missing apron; side-facing feet; chubby body; made by Georgene; circa 1938. $1,500-plus. (*Becky Mucchetti collection*)

Knickerbocker "Dress Me" Ann: 19 inches; clothes designed to be easily removed by a child; circa 1965. $165. (*Becky Mucchetti collection*)

Handmade Ann: 25 inches; wool hair, polyester legs, and sewn-on features; circa 1970. $25-35. (*Becky Mucchetti collection*)

Ann-Type Doll: 14 inches; made by Georgene after Knickerbocker gained the production rights; appears to be an effort to utilize leftover striped leg fabric; circa 1965. $95. (*Becky Mucchetti collection*)

Beloved Belindy: 18 inches; all original; made by Knickerbocker; circa 1964. $650-plus. (*Becky Mucchetti collection*)

Ann and Andy: 17 inches; Kusunoki/Phoenix Toy Companies; sold in Japan only; 1991; swivel heads; traditional feet. $300-350 pair. (*Bonnie and Larry Vaughan collection*)

Ann and Andy: 22 inches; unique design with swivel heads; Kusunoki/Phoenix Toy Companies; sold in Japan only; 1991. $500-550 for pair. (*Bonnie and Larry Vaughan collection*)

Raggedy Bears: 1.75 inches; fully jointed and carefully detailed; open edition; released in 1989 by artist Carol Stewart. $200 each.

Ann and Andy: 8 inches; painted muslin faces; cotton clothes; Ann 1985; Andy 1992; by Rebecca Iverson Swanson. $200 each. (*Becky Mucchetti collection*)

Heartbeat Ann: 17 inches; novelty item introduced in 1992; press the heart and hear a heartbeat; battery operated; Playschool, a subsidiary of Hasbro. $50-55. (*Bonnie and Larry Vaughan collection*)

Artist Raggedy Ann and Andy: 4 inches; cotton with painted features and yarn hair; made by Trudy Yelland; 1995. No price available.

Raggedy characters: 8 inches; camel with the wrinkled knees; Percy and Uncle Clem; muslin and cotton with painted faces; made 1986–1992; one of a kind dolls by Rebecca Iverson Swanson. $200 each. (*Becky Mucchetti collection*)

Artist Beloved Belindy: 4 inches; cotton with painted features; made by Trudy Yelland; 1995. No price available.

Raggedy Ann Awake/Asleep: 12 inches; made by Applause in 1996; this doll was designed by Raggedy artist Janie Jones upon Johnny Gruelle's grandson Kim's suggestion. The star print dress was first seen (and admired by the Gruelle's) when they saw it featured in the author's book "Enchanting Friends." $40.

Raggedy characters: 8 inches; Cleety, Beloved Belindy, and Dirty Faced Pirate; by Rebecca Iverson Swanson; 1992. $200 each. (*Becky Mucchetti collection*)

Raggedy Andy Awake/Asleep: 12 inches; made by Applause in 1996; limited edition. $40.

Quacky Doodles and Danny Doodles: 8.25 inches; made by Schoenhut; inspired by illustrations in the book written by Rose Hubbell and illustrated by Gruelle. Design date of 1915; missing hats. $400-500. (*Candy Brainard collection*)

Raggedy Ann and Andy bookends: 5.5 inches; cast iron; ©1931; P. F. Volland & Co. $100-150. (*Terri Kovacs collection*)

Birthday card: 3 x 5 inches; folds up so the birthday message appears in Ann's hands; marked "Volland." 1930s. $35-45. (*Terri Kovacs collection*)

Sunny Bunny book and character: 12 inches plus hat; mint-in-box condition; ©1918, P. F. Volland and Co., written by Nina Wilcox Putnam, illustrated by Johnny Gruelle; bunny also made by Volland; circa 1926, when Sunny Bunny became one of the Raggedy characters; mohair and felt. $1,000 set. (*Becky Mucchetti collection*)

Cut Raggedy Andy paper doll: Andy with several costumes and hats; Whitman; 1938. Sold with Ann and accessories.

Cut Raggedy Ann paper doll: Ann with several outfits and hats; Whitman; 1938. $65 for complete set.

Roly Poly: wooden toy: circa 1940; shows Ann in front of a house; no price available. (*Candy Brainard collection*)

Paper table and chair: part of the Raggedy Ann and Andy paper doll set; Whitman, 1938.

Reverse side of Roly Poly featuring Uncle Clem.

Raggedy Ann and Andy bowl: 9 inches; by Crooksville, ©1941. $95.

McCall's pattern with instructions for transfer designs and a child's size Raggedy quilt: most of the storybook characters are featured; © J. Gruelle; 1943. $25-35. (*Donna McPherson collection*)

Raggedy Ann and Andy paper dolls: Front cover of uncut book; printed by Saalfield; 1944. $150.

Back cover of paper doll book has Ann and Andy and Marcella and Beloved Belindy as well.

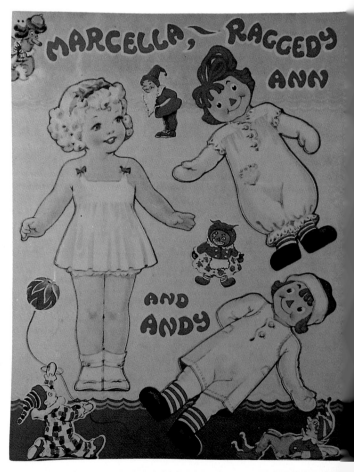

Kaleidoscope by Bobbs-Merrill: Ann is shown inside when the toy is turned; 1974. $95.

Ann and Andy umbrella: 24 inches in diameter; clear vinyl with Raggedy graphics by Bobbs-Merrill; 1980. $40-50. (*Bonnie and Larry Vaughan collection*)

Becky and Ann Figurine: 4 inches Made by Catherine McCullough; circa 1946; impressed with item's title and artist's name. $40-50. (*Becky Mucchetti collection*)

Raggedy Arthur pillow: 14 inches; character dog featured in the books; Bobbs-Merrill; 1978. $60-65. (*Bonnie and Larry Vaughan collection*)

Raggedy fabric: 2 yards; cotton; circa 1975. $45-50.

Enamel box; 2 inches; Raggedy Ann; made by Limoges; Raggedy Ann's eyes and mouth are imprinted inside; l990s. $150.

Enamel Box: 2 inches; Raggedy Andy; made by Limoges; l990s. $150.

U. S. postage stamp: Ann was honored with a 32-cent stamp, along with other classic dolls, in 1997.

China wall plaque: 6.5 inches; produced in Japan only; ©Macmillan; l990s. $25-30.

Chapter III
Hand in Hand with Winnie-the-Pooh

A. A. Milne and Christopher Robin

Of course, I knew when I wrote *Enchanting Friends* how disenchanted Christopher Robin was with his persona. I chose to ignore it for the focus of that book was not about personal angst. This book is not either, but circumstances have changed enough for me to at least touch on the subject.

In 1974, when Christopher's autobiography, *The Enchanted Places,* was published, the world was stunned to learn with how much bitterness he remembered his childhood. Among other resentments, he felt exploited and accused his father of gaining fame by riding on his son's shoulders and bringing to life that imaginative child's playtime. He recalled his father as a remote and cold man. However, Ann Thwaite, in her 1990 biography of A. A. Milne, showed data that suggested he was a more involved and loving father than Christopher remembered.

The man simply had a difficult time dealing with the remnants of a childhood he could not shake, for the public would not let him. He proved with the publication of two autobiographies that he could write as well as his father had and the books were successful. Yet Christopher Milne could not become anything other than what his father inadvertently created—a boy who visited Buckingham Palace, said his prayers, and had famous toy companions. P. G. Wodenhouse parodied A. A. Milne, as did Beachcomber, by writing:

> *"Hush! Hush! Nobody cares!/Christopher Robin/Has fallen downstairs."*

Unfortunately, for the lad, everybody *did* care and no matter what he did or did not accomplish, he would remain joined at the hip with Winnie-the-Pooh.

On Saturday, April 20, 1996 Christopher Robin died; at last laying his demons to rest. Intellectually I know that he was an old man of 75 years, but to me he will always and forever remain the little boy who went Hoppity Hop.

Christopher Robin Milne with Pooh photograph by Marcus Addams; 1928; hangs in the National Portrait Gallery, London.

Anne Darlington and Christopher Robin photograph and newspaper clipping of the first day of school. A. A. Milne came to love Anne as much as if she were his daughter. He dedicated the book *Now We Are Six* to her with the inscription "because she is so speshal." (*Photograph courtesy of Christie's, London*)

A. A. Milne, Christopher Robin, and Pooh photo taken in 1926 by Howard Coster; hangs in the National Portrait Gallery, London.

A selection of photographs of Christopher Robin and Anne Darlington; mostly taken at Cotchwood Farm, Sussex, close to the 100 "Aker" Wood. (*Photograph courtesy of Christie's, London*)

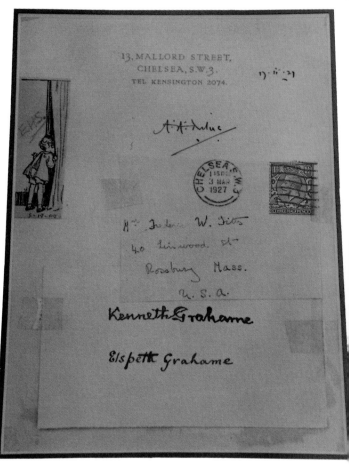

In 1927, Frederic Fitts of Roxbury, Massachusetts, asked A. A. Milne for his autograph. Milne signed his name on a sheet of his Mallord Street stationery and Kenneth and Elspeth Grahame also signed the paper. The sketch in the left-hand corner is from *When We Were Very Young.* The envelope, with a March 3, 1927, postmark, also appears to be in Milne's handwriting. (*Debby Birli collection*)

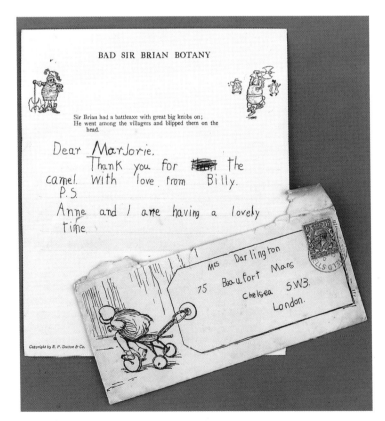

An autographed letter to Mrs. Darlington (Anne's Mother) from Christopher Robin. (*Photograph courtesy of Christie's, London*)

Hartfield as it appeared in 1906.

Ernest Howard Shepard

Winnie-the-Pooh floats high in the sky, lifted gracefully by a balloon. Christopher Robin descends the stairs, dragging Pooh in his wake. Pooh reaches high in the cupboard for a jar of honey. Most of us can evoke these images in our mind's eye. Clearly we see Pooh's rotund little body and enchanting face as he gazes with interest at the world around him. The man responsible for our mental impression of Pooh is Ernest H. Shepard—son, husband, father, painter of great talent, but remembered the most for his drawings of the world's most famous bear.

House in St. John's Wood. This residence, at 10 Kent Terrace figures prominently in E. H. Shepard's biography *Drawn from Memory.*

Framed print: "Hoppity" poem from *When We Were Very Young;* ©1924; limited edition, print number 120 of 250; initialed by E. H. Shepard; circa 1925.

Historical marker on E. H. Shepard's Kent Terrace house.

Ernest was born December 10, 1879, at 55 Springfield Road in the London section known as St. John's Wood. His father, Henry Donkin Shepard, and his mother, Jessie Harriet Lee, married in 1874 and became the parents of three children, Ernest and his siblings Cyril and Ethel. Henry was an architect and a remarkably good painter while Jessie was the daughter of a distinguished watercolorist. Exposed to a reverence for art on both sides of the family, Ernest was encouraged at an early age to define his innate artistic abilities. In fact, his father decided this should be his son's chosen career and showed the boy's early work to his artist friends with great pride. Ernest's introduction to classic art was found at his father's studio where a plaster cast of the Venus de Milo took center stage. The lad drew it over and over to gain proficiency.

The children had an extremely happy childhood with loving and attentive parents (even though all three were made to take violin lessons once a week!). And then the unthinkable happened, leaving a scar that remained for many years. When he was only ten, Ernest's mother died following a long illness.

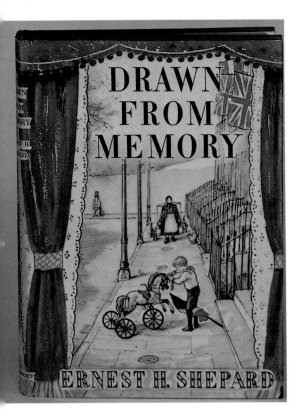

Book: *Drawn from Memory;* by E. H. Shepard; published by J. B. Lippincott in 1957. Shepard recounts a year in his life as a young lad of 6 or 7; a charming remembrance of Victorian England; drawn by the author as he remembered the events.

Finances plunged after her death, and the bereaved little group moved to the Shepard family home on Gordon Square with four maiden aunts. Years later Ernest wrote of his aunts with great affection in his autobiography, *Drawn from Memory.* The idyllic portrait he paints of his Victorian childhood was before his mother's untimely death when home was on the outskirts of Regents Park. He remembered with clarity the thoughts and feelings of a child and, because of this ability, the perception of him was of a perennial youth. This was far from the truth for Shepard was a serious professional and an astute businessman. He could write with a boyhood zest, but it should be realized that it was actually a child thinking and a *man* remembering. Life with the aunts continued for a year after which the little nuclear family made a move to Hammersmith. Unfortunately this house was ravaged during World War II and no longer stands.

The two boys were first enrolled at Oliver's in St. John's Wood, a school they both deplored. Since their father's brother was a senior master at St. Paul's, they were transferred to the prep school at this institution. Ernest enjoyed both Brewster's Prep and St. Paul's proper for he made friends easily, excelled at history, science, and English, and found time to play games as well.

He attended drawing classes two mornings a week and was fortunate to have a high master who paid attention to the aptitudes of his students. The master decided Ernest should work toward gaining a scholarship to the Royal Academy. St. Paul's art school was brilliantly run and quite early on the ability of Ernest Shepard was singled out. Because of this he spent Saturday's at Heatherly's Art School in final preparation for his scholarship attempt. He was 16, small for his age, and understandably felt at odds among the older bearded students. Following Queen Victoria's Jubilee he was informed that the Royal Academy had accepted him on probation. He submitted his drawings, passed, and spent the next three years tuition free. During his second year he entered three works for a Landseer Scholarship and won a place worth £40 for two years. While attending the school he became acquainted with Florence Chaplin, another clever student. She was three years older and, incidentally, the granddaughter of Ebeneezer Landell, artist and one of the founders of *Punch.*

In 1900, Ernest won the British Institution prize and at the age of 21 he rented a Chelsea studio with a fellow student. Shepard was an accomplished painter and sketcher who always worked from a model. Between 1900 and 1914 he illustrated a plethora of books. Among them were *Tom Brown, Toby, Aesop's Fables, Henry Esmond, Play the Game, Money or Wife, Smouldering Fires,* and the jacket for *David Copperfield.*

His father died in 1902 after suffering from disseminating sclerosis. Of course Ernest was grieved and never stopped missing him, but by this time he was forming a relationship with Florence Chaplin. They married in 1904 and made Arden Cottage in Surrey their first home. The couple's first child, Graham, was born in that house and they lived in it until just prior to their daughter, Mary's, birth on Christmas Day in 1909. Shepard's sketchbooks over the next years were full of studies of his beloved children.

Professionally he was fairly busy but hoped for a position with *Punch.* After sending several ideas a week to this periodical and having no success, he *finally* placed a drawing and by the start of World War I he was an established *Punch* artist.

Ernest Shepard's insight into children's imaginations was deft and sure. He always knew that it was a child's gift to bring toys to life. What a mistake we parents make when we dispose of our offspring's treasures because *we* feel it has been outgrown or, worse yet, *dirty.* The one person who all his life could capture the feelings of a youngster was Shepard. His own children's toys had character much in the way Christopher Robin's did. It was probably why the two men, he and Milne, (who didn't have much else in common) could work so successfully together. Once when Ernest was home alone, while his family vacationed, he wrote a letter to seven-year-old Graham telling him that his teddy bear "Growler" had been an awful nuisance talking and jabbering all night.

Many years before, during Victoria's Diamond Jubilee, there had been a long military parade. Although Ernest had a fascination for the pomp and circumstance he, at that moment, decided this was not a career he wanted to pursue. When the

Boer War started in 1899 he never felt the slightest impulse to volunteer. However, World War I affected him more deeply and the second half of 1915 found him being trained as an officer. He was commissioned on December, 15, went into action, and came home unscathed. His brother Cyril was not so lucky and was killed in the first attack at Somme.

At the war's end Shepard went back to *Punch* as a contributor and was invited to be on the regular staff in 1921. E. V. Lucas, a man of letters and also a director at Methuen Publishing Company, worked at *Punch* as well. He suggested that Shepard do some drawings for a book of verses that A. A. Milne was currently working on entitled *When We Were Very Young*. At the onset Milne was not impressed for he wanted an illustrator as famous as himself. However when he saw the eleven drawings for the book (that first appeared in *Punch)* he was convinced. A. A. Milne hereafter embraced Shepard's work with wholehearted enthusiasm, insisting that he also draw for his next book, *Winnie-the-Pooh*. To this end, Ernest traveled to Milne's home, Cotchford Farm, to meet Christopher Robin and the toys. He wandered around Ashdown Forest to get the feel of the place and also did some preliminary sketches. Although most of the animals were drawn (with minor alterations) as they appeared in reality, Shepard had used "Growler" as the teddy model in the first book. He decided to keep on doing so for he preferred his own son's bear.

When sales confirmed the success of the partnership, Milne wrote for publication the following compliment:

> "*When I am gone/Let Shepard decorate my tomb/and put (if there is room)/Two pictures on the stone:/Piglet from page a hundred and eleven/ And Pooh and Piglet walking (157).../And Peter, thinking they are my own/Will welcome me into heaven.*"

Yet the two were never close and the artist once said he always had to start over when working with the writer.

For the following decade, Shepard had so much work he found himself at last making a substantial living. Now it was possible to build a "dream house" for his wife and children. A location near Guilford was chosen, but shortly before the home was completed a tragedy struck—Florence suddenly died. Graham and Mary never knew what happened. Shepard could not discuss it and offered no explanations. His wife had entered the hospital for tests and abruptly collapsed. The disaster was total for his son, a twenty-year-old college student, Mary, seventeen, and Ernest, himself a man in his prime. The little group moved into the new house anyway and at first life was pretty grim.

The years passed and Ernest, having his work to sustain him, finally reached a period with some semblance of normality. When Graham married Anne Gibbon, a Canadian girl, he bought them a house in St. John's Wood not far from where he was born. In 1937, Mary married E. V. Lucas, her father's colleague at *Punch*.

Graham, a reservist, was called into service in 1939, whereupon Anne and Shepard's only grandchild, Minette, departed for safer ground in Canada. They took "Growler" with them (the bear that Ernest had once described as magnificent, having never seen the like.) "Growler" ended his life in his new country, meeting his unfortunate demise in the mouth of a dog. In August of 1943, Graham returned home for a short furlough. Six weeks later his ship went down in the Atlantic with him aboard. Shepard's reaction to grief was to ignore it in the true Victorian mode of behavior. No breast beating for him, but inside the blow was insupportable.

The following November, after many years of being alone, Shepard married Norah Carroll. It was a happy union and the two eventually located in West Sussex in a house called Woodmancote. They spent the rest of their lives there as content as could be expected. In the next decade, besides writing his childhood memories, *Drawn from Memory*, he also illustrated a variety of books about Pooh. Privately he admitted to friends that he was getting sick of that silly old bear. In spite of his feelings, the 1960s brought the highest financial returns from his association with Pooh. In 1972, news of the extent of his works and fame was finally recognized by Whitehall. Seventy-one years after his first exhibition at the Royal Academy, Ernest Howard Shepard was awarded the Order of the British Empire.

Shepard did his last work for Pooh when he was over ninety. Advanced age brought on deafness, but he minded his failing eyesight the most. Sadly he died in 1976 during preparations for the "silly old bear's" fiftieth anniversary. Biographer Rawle Knox describes Shepard's work as having a clarity of line, a Vermeer-like consciousness of light, a nice judgment for vignette boundaries, and a genius for detail. Knox was not a Pooh fan, but he, like so many others, could see that *nothing* could ever replace Ernest Shepard's inspired drawings.

E. H. Shepard's home in Lodsworth, West Sussex.

The "Woodmancote" sign on the brick fence.

This preliminary sketch by E. H. Shepard was rendered when the artist first encountered the animals in 1924. Note that Pooh is drawn as he actually appeared before the changes were made. (*Courtesy of the Victoria and Albert Museum, London*)

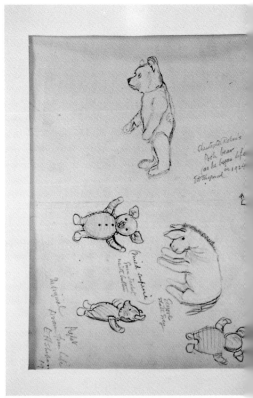

Original sketch by E. H. Shepard: first drawing for the frontispiece of *Winnie-the-Pooh*. (*Courtesy of the Victoria and Albert Museum, London*)

Sketch by E. H. Shepard: 3.5 x 5 inches; an original illustration for "Hunting the Woozle," published in *Winnie-the-Pooh*, 1926, Page 34; ink; not framed; sold at Christie's, London in December 1996. $59,400. (*Photo courtesy of Christie's, London*)

Sketch by E. H. Shepard: 4.5 x 3.75 inches; an original illustration for "Hunting the Woozle," published in *Winnie-the-Pooh*, 1926, Page 37; pen and ink; not framed; sold at Christie's, London in December 1996. $49,500. (*Photo courtesy of Christie's, London*)

Sketch by E. H. Shepard: 6.5 x 8.5 inches; an original illustration for "Hunting the Woozle" published in *Winnie-the-Pooh*, 1926, Page 34; pen and ink; signed with initials; not framed; sold at Christie's, London in December 1996. $115,500. (*Photo courtesy of Christie's, London*)

Sketch by E. H. Shepard: 3.5 x 5 inches; *Winnie-the-Pooh*, Page 38, pen and ink, not framed; sold at Christie's, London in December 1996. $85,800. (*Photo courtesy of Christie's, London*)

71

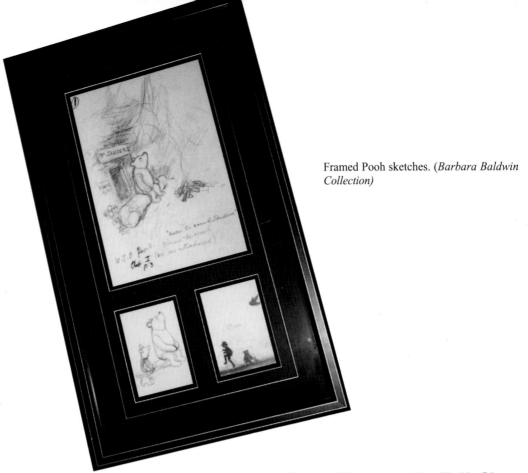

Framed Pooh sketches. (*Barbara Baldwin Collection*)

Books Illustrated by E. H. Shepard

The following seven books were illustrated between 1900 and 1914:

Tom Brown's School Days. Hughes
David Copperfield. Dickens
Aesop's Fables. Rhymes by Henslow
Henry Esmond. Thackeray
Play the Game. Avery
Money or Wife. Rowlands
Smouldering Fires. Green
Everybody's Book of the Queen's Doll House. (end papers) ed. Benson and Weaver. 1924
When We Were Very Young. Milne. 1925
Playtime and Company. Lucas. 1925
A Book of Children's Verses. Doran. 1925
The Holly Tree and Other Stories. Dickens. 1925
The King's Breakfast. Milne. 1925
Winnie-the-Pooh. Milne. 1926
The Little One's Log. Erleigh. 1927
Now We Are Six. Milne. 1927
Lets Pretend. Agnew. 1927
Fun and Fantasy. Edited by E. H. S. 1927
Mr. Punch's County Soup. Lucas. 1928
The House at Pooh Corners. Milne. 1928
The Golden Age-Kenneth Graham. Dodd. 1928
Livestock in Barracks. Armstrong. 1929
Everybody's Boswell. ed. Morley. 1930
Dream Days. Grahame. 1930
When I Was Very Young. Milne. 1930
The Wind in the Willows. Grahame. 1931
Christmas Poems. Drinkwater. 1931
Sycamore Square. Struthers. 1932

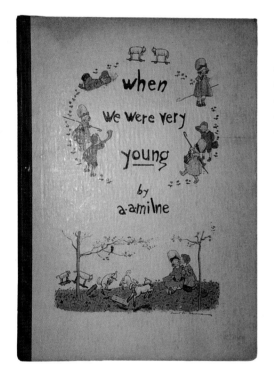

Book: *When We Were Very Young,* 7.25 x 10 inches; special holiday edition of October 1925; reprinted twice more the same month; E. P. Dutton & Co. $350-plus. (*Nadine Gravatt collection*)

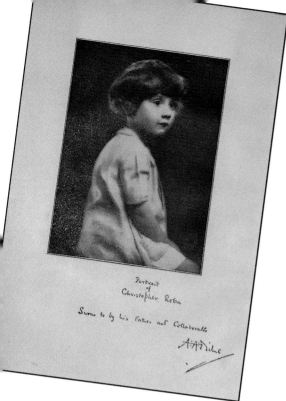

Christopher Robin portrait in frontispiece of the holiday edition of *When We Were Very Young*.

The Christopher Robin Verses. Milne. 1932
Bevis. Jefferies. 1932
Everybody's Lamb. ed. Ward. 1933
The Cricket in the Cage. Chalmers. 1933
Victoria Regina. Housman. 1934
Perfume from Provence. Fortescue. 1935
The Seventh Daughter. Todd. 1935
The Modern Struwelpeter. Struther. 1936
As the Bee Sucks. Lucas. 1937
Cheddar Gorge. Housman. 1937
The Golden Sovereign. Housman. 1937
Sunset House. (Frontispiece) Fortescue.
The Reluctant Dragon. Grahame. 1938
Gracious Majesty. Housman. 1941
Bertie's Escapade. Grahame. 1949
The Islanders. Pertwee. 1950
Enter David Garrick. Stewart. 1951
Year In, Year Out. Milne. 1952
The Silver Curlew. Farjeon. 1953
Susan, Bill and the Wolf Dog. Saville. 1954
The Brownies and Other Stories. Ewing. 1954
The Cuckoo Clock. Malesworth. 1954
The Golden Age. Grahame. 1954
Dream Days. Grahame. 1954
The Glass Slipper. Farjeon. 1955
Susan, Bill and the Vanishing Boy. Saville. 1955
Frogmorton. Colling. 1955
Modern Fairy Tales. ed. Green. 1955
Susan, Bill and the Golden Clock. Saville. 1955
The Crystal Mountain. Rough. 1956
The Secret Garden. Burnett. 1956
Susan, Bill and the "Saucey Kate." Saville. 1956
Royal Reflections. Goulden. 1956

Book: *The House-at-Pooh-Corner* by A. A. Milne; ©Methuen Co. Ltd., London, 1928; this beautiful edition is bound in burgundy leather with the Shepard characters and end papers in gilt. $700.

Book: *The King's Breakfast*; song book by A. A. Milne with music by H. Fraser-Simson; decorations by Ernest H. Shepard, published in 1925 by McClelland & Stewart Ltd., Toronto. $125.

Song book: *The Hums of Pooh* by A. A. Milne; music by H. Fraser-Simson; decorations by E. H. Shepard, E. P. Dutton & Co. Inc. ©1930. $150-plus.

The Christopher Robin Birthday Book: A. A. Milne with E. H. Shepard drawings. Methuen Co. Ltd., London. ©1930. Verses and drawings from all four books on each day of the year; cloth cover with gilt design. $150.

The Christopher Robin calendar: verses by A. A. Milne; decorations by E. H. Shepard; published by Methuen Co. Ltd., London, in 1929; complete with mailing envelope. $750.

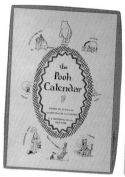

Pooh calendars published in 1930 by
Methuen Co. Ltd., London, and E. P.
Dutton, New York: Dutton version comes in
the box shown on left and Methuen's has
original paper mailing envelope; first and
only editions. $750.

At the Back of the North Wind. MacDonald. 1956
Susan, Bill and the Dark Stranger. Saville. 1956
Tom Brown's School Days. Hughes. 1956
The World of Pooh. Milne. 1957
Drawn from Memory. Shepard. 1957
*The Pancake. e*d. Fassett. 1957
The World of Christopher Robin. 1958
Old Greek Fairy tales. Green. 1958
Briar Rose. Fassett. 1958
Drawn from Life. Shepard. 1961
Hans Christian Anderson. Trans. Kingsland. 1961
*A Noble Company. e*d. Compton. 1961
The Flattered Flying Fish. Rieu. 1962
Ben and Brock. Shepard. 1965
The Pooh Story Book. Milne. 1965
Betsy and Joe. Shepard. 1966
The Christopher Robin Verse Book. Milne. 1967
The Wind in the Willows. Grahame. 1971
The House at Pooh Corners (full color.) Milne. 1974

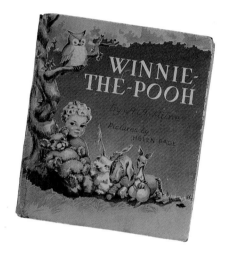

Winnie-the-Pooh book: hard cover; A. A.
Milne; illustrations by Helen Page; published
by John Martin's House Inc., 1946. $95.

Coloring book: paper edition; ©1960 by
Stephen Slesinger Inc., Shepard illustrations.
$50-75. (*Elena Sodano collection*)

Golden Shape Books: *Winnie-the-Pooh,*
©1964 and 1965; Tigger, ©1968; W. Disney.
$35-45. (*Lois Harvey collection*)

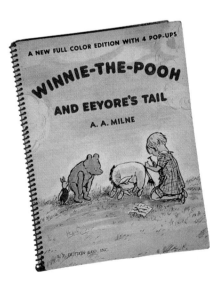

Book: *Winnie-the-Pooh and Eeyore's Tail*; A.
A. Milne; E. H. Shepard drawings; full color
with pop-up pages; published by E. P.
Dutton in the 1950s. $195-plus.

W. Disney song book: includes "Winnie the
Pooh;" ©1963 Wonderland Music Co. $50.
Roo: 9 inches; plush; made for Sears; 1960s.
$20-25. (*Lois Harvey collection*)

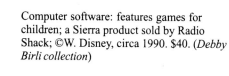

Computer software: features games for children; a Sierra product sold by Radio Shack; ©W. Disney, circa 1990. $40. (*Debby Birli collection*)

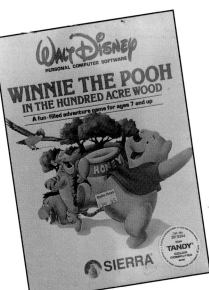

Winnie the Pooh record: LP record in a sleeve that also contains a fully illustrated book; ©1965 W. Disney Productions. $45-50.

Poohsticks rules booklet: Official rules for playing Poohsticks; available from the Corner Shop in Hartfield, England. $25.

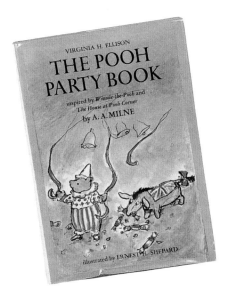

The Pooh Party Book: by Virginia Ellison, inspired by A. A. Milne; illustrated by E. H. Shepard; published by E. P. Dutton & Co., New York ©1971; recipes and party games. $45-50.

Russian language *Winnie-the-Pooh*: paperback format; 1980s. $34-45. (*Lori Woo collection*)

Read-along books with records: *Winnie the Pooh and the Honey Tree*, ©1976, W. Disney. $45-50. *Winnie the Pooh and the Blustery Day*, ©W. Disney. $45-50. (*Lois Harvey collection*)

Breton language *Winnie-the-Pooh*: paperback edition; 1950s. $35-40. (*Lori Woo collection*)

The students at Berea State Teachers College in Kentucky started making toys from commercial patterns in the 1920s as a fundraiser. It is believed that a Pooh set was a part of the project. Rabbit: 8.5 inches; label sewn on bottom and sticker label on one side; circa 1930. $75. (*Becky Mucchetti collection*)

Kanga and Roo: 12 inches; brown and white mohair; glass eyes; British; circa 1920; childhood toy of Anne Darlington (1919-1958), friend and inseparable companion to Christopher Robin Milne; sold along with ephemera at Christie's auction, December 1995. (*Photograph courtesy of Christie's, London*)

Pooh: 17 inches; made by the Teddy Toy Co., England; circa 1930. $1,000. (*Romy Roeder collection*)

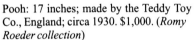

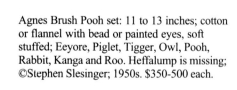

Agnes Brush Pooh set: 11 to 13 inches; cotton or flannel with bead or painted eyes, soft stuffed; Eeyore, Piglet, Tigger, Owl, Pooh, Rabbit, Kanga and Roo. Heffalump is missing; ©Stephen Slesinger; 1950s. $350-500 each.

Piglet: 4 inches; felt; unknown maker; possibly of British origins. No price available. (*Richard Wright collection/ Photo by Anne Jackson*)

Kanga and Roo: 12 inches; velvet with embroidered features; kapok stuffed; probably British; circa 1940. $90. (*Maria Bluni collection*)

Below: Christopher Robin and Pooh: 8.5 inches, by Muriel Bruyere; circa 1940; modeled head, arms, feet (and Pooh); cloth body and legs; hand-fashioned smock and short pants. $400. (*Becky Mucchetti collection*)

Probable British Pooh: 15 inches; plush with glass eyes; jointed but arms move together; circa 1950. $250-350. (*Elsa Malcom collection*)

Pooh: 13 inches; made by Agnes Brush, 1950s; with original hang tag; ©Stephen Slesinger Inc. $450-plus. (*Becky Mucchetti collection*)

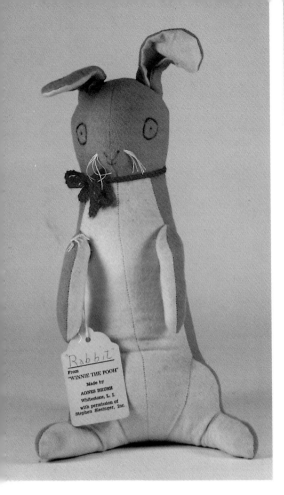

Rabbit: 11 inches; made by Agnes Brush, 1950s; original hang tag; ©Stephen Slesinger Inc. $450. (*Becky Mucchetti collection*)

Plush Pooh: 9 inches; bell in ear; red felt mouth; not jointed; tagged "J. Swedlin/ Gund;" 1964. $50-60. Plush Tigger: 11 inches; googlie eyes; tagged "J. Swedlin/ Gund;" ©W. Disney; 1964–1968. $50-60. (*Lois Harvey collection*)

Pooh nightdress case: 14 inches; mohair head, hands, and feet attached to a satin and velvet case; "Pooh" printed on pillow; made by Merrythought, England, in the 1960s; ©W. Disney. $1,000.

Schuco Winnie-the-Pooh; mohair with glass eyes and a vinyl nose; circa 1960. No price available. (*Barbara Baldwin collection*)

Pooh characters: Pooh, Kanga and Roo, Rabbit, Piglet, Tigger, and Eeyore; made in velvet by Gund; ©W. Disney; 1966. $50-80 each. (*Becky Mucchetti collection*)

Pooh puppet: 12 inches; tan felt and button eyes; made by Determined Productions Inc.; missing red jacket; 1960s. $145-155.

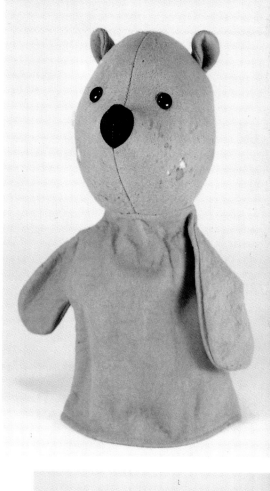

The Woozle: 6 inches; velveteen with felt features and hat; made by Gund; ©W. Disney; 1965. $50-80. (*Lori Woo collection*)

Heffalump: 6 inches; velveteen with striped shirt and felt hat; made by Gund; ©W. Disney; 1965. $50-80. (*Lori Woo collection*)

Pooh: 10 inches; plush with glass eyes, removable sweater, sewn-on hat, yarn nose, and airbrushed feet; made by Gund; 1964; label in seam; ©W. Disney. $350.

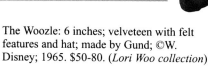

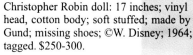

Heffalump: 6 inches; velveteen with felt stripes and features, net wings; made by Gund; ©W. Disney; 1965. $50-80. (*Lori Woo collection*)

Christopher Robin doll: 17 inches; vinyl head, cotton body; soft stuffed; made by Gund; missing shoes; ©W. Disney; 1964; tagged. $250-300.

English Merrythought Eeyore: 13 inches; mohair and shaggy plush mane, plastic eyes, tagged on foot; ©W. Disney; 1960s. $300.

English Merrythought Pooh: 14 inches; gold mohair; red felt top with "Pooh" painted on; tagged on foot; ©W. Disney; 1960s. $625-plus.

Pooh's friend Piglet: 10 inches plus ears; flesh-colored flannel with plastic eyes; soft stuffed; removable flannel clothes; made in England by Merrythought; excellent condition; ©W. Disney; 1960s. $400.

English Merrythought Tigger: 10 inches; striped short plush, glass eyes; quite accurately resembles the original animal owned by Christopher Robin; ©W. Disney; 1960s. $300-plus.

English Pooh: 24 inches; made by Merrythought; mohair with plastic eyes; missing shirt; ©W. Disney; circa 1966. $700-plus.

Christopher Robin and Pooh: 7 inches and 5 inches; hand made; 1960s or 1970s. $45 pair. (*Becky Mucchetti collection*)

Eeyore: 14 inches; hand made of corduroy with pasted-on features; button-on tail, 1960s; McCall's pattern. $65.

Tigger: 16 inches; plush with plastic eyes and nose; made by Gund for Sears; 1970s. ©W. Disney. $85.

Kanga: 12 inches; Berea College project; Roo missing; 1970s. Berea animals are always made from calico. $55. (*Becky Mucchetti collection*)

Plush Pooh: 10 inches; no joints; made by Gund for Sears; 1970s-1980s; ©W. Disney. $40.

Artist Pooh bear: 11 inches; plush version of Pooh by artist Flora Mediate; all jointed; removable red vest; 1983. $110.

R. John Wright Pooh: 14 inches; gold mohair; bee on right ear; green satin ribbon sash with gold printing; made in a limited edition for the first Teddy Bear Convention at Disney World in 1988; ©W. Disney. $1,600.

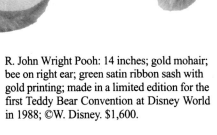

Pooh and friends: 3 to 5 inches each, flocked set of small characters made for Sears, 1988; ©W. Disney. $25-35 each. (*Elsa Malcom collection*)

Eeyore, Pooh, and Tigger: 7, 9, and 10 inches; made for Disneyland Stores, ©W. Disney. $35 each. (*Lois Harvey collection*)

Christopher Robin and Pooh: 14 inches; muslin with painted face; wearing blue trousers and smock, hat, socks, and sandals; felt bear with jointed limbs; made by Rebecca Iverson Swanson, ©1986. $600. (*Photo courtesy of Becky Mucchetti*)

Pooh with "hunny" pot: 14 inches, limited edition of 5,000 by R. John Wright, 1989, wears bib and has a bee in his ear; bee is hand made of felt; mint-in-box condition; ©W. Disney. $650-plus.

Pooh: 13 inches, 1970s design by Anne Wilkinson; ©W. Disney. $175-plus.

Owl: 10 inches, Anne Wilkinson designs; ©W. Disney; 1970s. $150.

Eeyore, Tigger, and Piglet: 11, 10, and 6 inches; discontinued Anne Wilkinson Design Toys; all with original labels and tags; part of a complete set; ©W. Disney; 1970s. $150-250 each.

Christopher Robin: 19 inches, made by Anne Wilkinson in the 1970s; discontinued and out of business in the 1990s; ©W. Disney. $250-plus.

Kanga and Roo: 11 inches; designed by Anne Wilkinson in the 1970s; ©W. Disney. $150-250.

Pooh, 5.25 inches, made in limited edition of 100 for 1991 Disney World Convention in Florida by artist Carol Stewart; tagged and signed on back of shirt. ©W. Disney. $425.

Pooh: 3 inches; 1990 Disney convention piece; limited edition of 100; by Carol Stewart; ©W. Disney. $350.

Rabbit: 12 inches; designed by Anne Wilkinson in the 1970s. The rabbit is one of the hardest to find in the series; ©W. Disney. $150-250.

Piglets: 3.5 and 6 inches; made by Anne Wilkinson; all cotton; ©W. Disney; 1992. $25-30.

Pooh on a stick; 14 inches; Anne Wilkinson designs; fabric toy that can be popped in and out of the cylinder by manipulating the stick; ©W. Disney. $75.

Piglet on a stick: 19 inches; Anne Wilkinson design; all cotton; Piglet disappears inside the cone; ©W. Disney; 1990s. $35-40.

Tigger: 9 inches; made by Ann Wilkinson; all cotton; ©W. Disney; 1992. $35-40.

Eeyore: 6 inches; made by Anne Wilkinson; all cotton; ©W. Disney; 1992.. $35-40.

Pooh: 12 inches; made by Anne Wilkinson, England; discontinued in about 1993; cotton with felt vest; ©W. Disney. $75-80.

English Gabrielle Pooh. Winnie the Pooh and accessories; comes in presentation box that may be used as a display; complete with wooden table, chair, and tablecloth, made in conjunction with Royal Doulton who fashioned the classic decorated china cup, plate, and wall clock; Gabrielle Designs Ltd., 1995. ©W. Disney. $250-275.

Pooh: 12 inches; designed by Terry and Doris Michaud for the 1993 Disney World Bear Convention; limited edition of 100 pieces; mohair with flannel nightshirt and cap; ©W. Disney; mint-in-box condition with enamel pin and certificate. $475-plus.

Winnie the Pooh and Piglet: 11 inches and 6 inches; boxed set by Gabrielle Designs, England; limited edition of 2,000 pieces; 1994; imaginatively and attractively boxed to resemble Pooh sticks bridge; Pooh holds a stick with edition numbers imprinted on it; Shepard graphics on box cover; ©W. Disney. $250-300.

Winnie the Pooh: 11 inches; classic Pooh by Gabrielle, England; Pooh wears a knit vest and has a "hunny" pot; limited edition of 2,000 in 1994; in presentation box; ©W. Disney. $200-250.

Winnie the Pooh: 2 inches; one-of-a-kind the artist made for herself; 1996. April Whitcomb Gustafson is one of the first artists working in miniatures to gain international recognition. (*Courtesy of April Whitcomb Gustafson*)

Steiff Winnie the Pooh: 12 inches; made expressly for the 1994 Teddy Bear Convention at Disney World; limited edition of 2,500; gold mohair with a knit vest. ©W. Disney. $800-900.

Pocket Eeyore: 6 inches; the third animal in the pocket series; designed and produced by R. John Wright; limited edition of 3,500 pieces; tagged and in presentation box; ©W. Disney, 1995. $280 at issue.

Pocket Pooh and Piglet: 5 inches and 2.5 inches; by R. John Wright in a limited edition of 250 pieces for F. A. O. Schwarz; called "Wintertime Pooh and Piglet;" ©W. Disney; 1994. $1,200-plus.

Piglet: 1.75 inches; cotton velvet with painted metal eyes; leather or ultra-suede ears; open edition for the 1996 Disney convention; by Carol Stewart; ©W. Disney. $200 at issue.

Pooh's house: 20 x 16 x 14 inches; 1996 Disney auction piece; one of a kind; complete miniature house encased in an oak cabinet; Pooh has an overstuffed velvet chair; brass bed with quilt; corner cupboard, hutch with jars of honey, table and chairs, rocker, carpet, brick fireplace, and stool. Room is electrically wired and enhanced with hardwood floors, wood wainscoting, and beamed ceiling. Came with a 3-inch Pooh and a 1.75-inch Piglet; by Carol Stewart; ©W. Disney. Price realized at auction: $16,000.

Artist "Winniebear:" 5.5 inches; gold mohair; felt vest varies in color; entirely hand made by artist Victoria Beaumont-Marsden of Scotland; 1996. $90-100.

Artists Lin and John Van Houten holding two versions of their distinctive Pooh-type teddies. $1996. $250-plus each.

Prototype Owl and Rabbit: 11 inches; Gabrielle Designs; ©W. Disney, 1996.

Pooh with book: 9 inches, made by Gabrielle Designs; 1996; limited edition of 2,500 pieces; comes with a mahogany plinth and a miniature version of the book by A. A. Milne. ©W. Disney. $200.

R. John Wright pocket Tigger: 4 inches; felt; all jointed; limited edition; 1996; ©W. Disney; tagged and in presentation box. $290 at issue.

Pocket Christopher Robin and Pooh: 11 inches and 6 inches; made by R. John Wright; 1997. $1,325 at issue. Christopher Robin is also sold without Pooh; ©W. Disney; issue price of $895. (*Photo courtesy of R. John Wright*)

Pooh and friends: 10, 16, 17, and 20 inches; one-of-a-kind set made by Canterbury Bears for the 1996 auction at Disney world; ©W. Disney. Price realized $3,700. (*Photo courtesy of Maude and John Blackburn*)

Christmas Ornaments: 3 inches; set of five flocked figures; ©W. Disney; made for Sears in the 1970s. $10-15 each.

Nursery Pottery Jug: 4 inches The middle of three sizes of jugs made by Ashtead Pottery. Illustrations are Christopher Robin with fishing pole and the words "That's What I'm Doing--Newting." Also illustrates Christopher with a butterfly net (under the spout) *Emmeline is* on the reverse side. On the bottom is printed "This is No. 11 of 24 pieces of the Christopher Robin Nursery Set made in England by Ashtead Potters Ltd. Epsom from E. H. Shepard's Copyright Designs. Reg. No 740058." 1920s. $500.

Reverse side of Ashtead Jug.

Ashtead Pottery chocolate cup with lid. The reverse shows Pooh getting honey out of his cupboard; 1920s. $500. (*Barbara Baldwin collection*)

Ashtead Pottery Plate: 7 inches; showing Pooh on a limb with honey jars; 1920s. $500 (*Barbara Baldwin collection*)

Ashtead Pottery Bowl: 5 inches; No. 5 of 24 pieces of the nursery set; 1920s. $500 (*Barbara Baldwin collection*)

Ashtead Pottery cup and saucer: one of 24 pieces; 1920s. $500. (*Barbara Baldwin collection*)

Cup: 2.75 inches high; pottery cup with Pooh embossed on two sides; made by Krueger for Stephen Slesinger; circa 1940. $125.

Bowl: 5 inches diameter; pottery bowl with Pooh embossed five times to form scalloped edge; made by Krueger for Stephen Slesinger; circa 1940. $125.

Pooh pitcher: 4.5 inches; made by Krueger, Germany, for Stephen Slesinger; circa 1940 $125. (*Barbara Baldwin collection*)

Winnie-the-Pooh bowl: 5.5 inches; part of a three-piece nursery set; (other pieces also shown) ©Stephen Slesinger; made in Germany; circa 1950. $125-150.

Winnie-the-Pooh mug: 3 inches; two-handled; showing Christopher Robin nailing on Eeyore's tail while Pooh watches; ©Stephen Slesinger; made in Germany by Krueger; circa 1950. $125-150.

Winnie-the-Pooh pitcher: 2.5 inch, circa 1950; more simplistic than earlier china with this theme; ©Stephen Slesinger; made in Germany by Krueger. $125-150.

Cup and saucer: entitled "The Woozle;" made by Royal Doulton; ©W. Disney; 1996. $25-35.

Cup and saucer: entitled "The Rescue;" made by Royal Doulton; ©W. Disney; 1996. $25-35.

Mugs, made in England, ©W. Disney; 1996. $10-15 each.

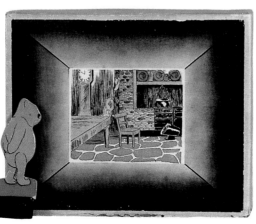

Winnie-the-Pooh nursery set. Presented in a box that resembles a book. Inner box has a kitchen scene on one side and the 100 "aker" woods on the other. Inside is a book and stand-up characters so that children may engage in play while being read to. Methuen; 1931. $450-plus.

Room scenes from the nursery set.

Winnie-the-Pooh game: Colorful board with four characters, Pooh, Piglet, Rabbit, and Christopher Robin Instructions printed on the lid of the box; Parker Brothers Inc.; 1959 ©Stephen Slesinger Inc., New York. $125-150.

Winnie-the-Pooh wooden figures: Christopher Robin, Piglet, Tigger, Eeyore, Squirrel, Owl, two rabbits, and a jointed Pooh; registry number on smallest rabbit; English; circa 1935. $285-300.

The board and game pieces. From the 1959 Parker Bros. Game.

Musical crib mobile: 12 inches; plastic umbrella with all the characters hanging from nylon threads; made for Sears; 1963; ©W. Disney. $125-150. (*Lois Harvey collection*)

Pooh and honey pot cookie jar: 11 inches; Pooh sits holding a honey pot; made for Sears; ©W. Disney; circa 1970. $200-225.

Pooh fabric: 2 yards. Cotton; Pooh and several of the animals; Disney version; circa 1965; ©W. Disney. $45-50.

Pooh glass light fixture shade: 15 inches square. Frosted glass with colorful Pooh and friends all around the edges; circa 1970; ©W. Disney. $125.

Vinyl squeeze toy: 13 inches; made by Holland Hall; circa 1966; jointed arms and legs; ©W. Disney. $50-60. (*Elsa Malcom collection*)

Pooh and bee cookie jar: 11 inches; ceramic; made for Sears; Pooh holds a honey pot and a bee is on his head; the entire head forms the lid; ©W. Disney; circa 1970. $200-225.

Tigger cookie jar: 12 inches; the tiger holds a basket inscribed "Cookies;" his head forms the lid; Sears; ©W. Disney; circa 1970. $225-250.

Hooked rug: 38 x 47 inches; made by The Nantucket Collection; designed by Claire Murray; ©W. Disney; 1980s. $350.

Pooh cookie jar: 11 inches; showing Pooh holding a cookie; made by Metlox. $150.

Child's sweater: Size medium (20 to 25 pounds) made for Sears; 1980s; ©W. Disney. $15.

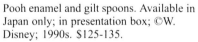

Decorative Pooh: 7.5 inches; resin molded and sculpted to look like wood; made by Charpente; ©W. Disney; circa 1993. $45-50. (*Katie Vogan collection*)

Pooh enamel box: .75 inches. Made by Crummles; England. Enamel with graphic of Pooh and a honey pot; discontinued about 1990; ©Berne Convention. $85-95.

Pooh enamel napkin ring: 1.25 inches; English enamel made by Crummles; Pooh with honey pot in various poses; discontinued about 1990; ©Berne Convention. $100-125.

Pooh enamel and gilt spoons. Available in Japan only; in presentation box; ©W. Disney; 1990s. $125-135.

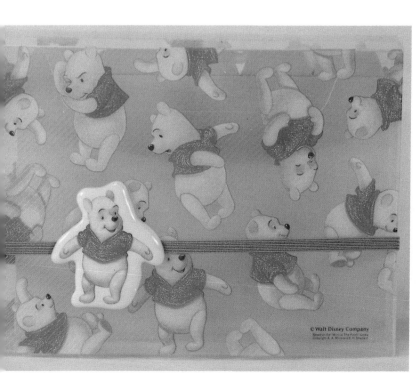

Pooh file case: index size; Japan only; ©W. Disney; l990s. $25-35.

Roly Poly. Made by Arco; ©W. Disney; circa 1990. $30-40. (*Elsa Malcom collection*)

Pooh enameled boxes. Made by Halcyon
Days; England; 1995; ©W. Disney. $100.

Pooh enameled boxes; made by Halcyon
Days; England; 1995; ©W. Disney.

Pooh enameled boxes: Made by Halcyon
Days; England; 1995; ©W. Disney. $100-150.

Pooh enameled box: made by Halcyon Days;
England; 1995; ©W. Disney. $150.

Pooh enameled boxes: made by Halcyon
Days; England; 1995; ©W. Disney The
boxes made by this company (a division of
Battersee Enamels) are also decorated all
around the sides. $100-150.

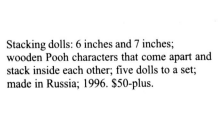

Stacking dolls: 6 inches and 7 inches;
wooden Pooh characters that come apart and
stack inside each other; five dolls to a set;
made in Russia; 1996. $50-plus.

Pooh picture frame: 2.5 x 3.5 inches; 1996; ©W. Disney; made by Charpente; ceramic Pooh and rabbit. $25.

Ceramic picture frame: 3 inches; 1996; ©W. Disney; made by Charpente. $25.

Canadian first-day cover. Canceled in White River, Ontario, on October 1, 1996. Sold out swiftly.

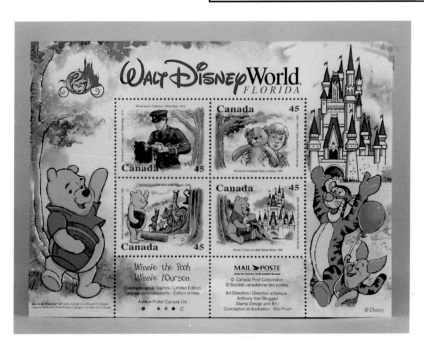

Canadian stamps: set of four stamps commemorating Winnie the Pooh; stamps include Captain Harry Coleburn and the real bear called Winnie; Christopher Robin and Pooh, classic Pooh and friends, and Disney Pooh. First issued October, 1996.

T-shirt: Classic Pooh and friends are pictured; issued by the Canadian Postal Service in conjunction with the commemorative stamps; 1996. $40-45.

Doll-size umbrella: classic Shepard design featuring Pooh, Christopher Robin, and all the other animals; ©W. Disney; 1997. $12-15.

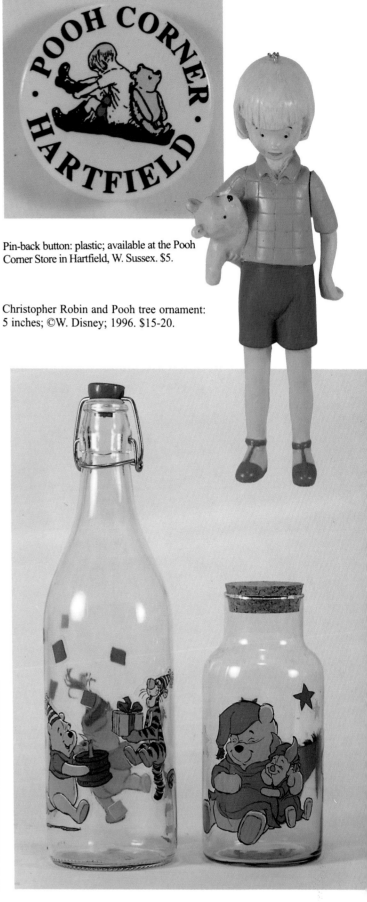

Pin-back button: plastic; available at the Pooh Corner Store in Hartfield, W. Sussex. $5.

Christopher Robin and Pooh tree ornament: 5 inches; ©W. Disney; 1996. $15-20.

Pooh bottles: 7 inches and 12 inches; hand decorated with window transfers; 1996. $8

Needlepoint Christmas stocking showing Christopher Robin and Pooh; velvet backing; 1996; ©W. Disney. $45-50.

Pooh bottles: 12 inches; hand decorated with window decorations; a variety of characters are used; 1996. $8-10 each.

Who's Pooh? Prototypes made at Gabrielle Designs, England, before selecting final bear to be used with Christopher Robin doll.

Pooh Christmas ornament: satin; made by Gibson; ©W. Disney. $5-10.

Pooh storage at Gabrielle Designs.

Assembling Poohs at Gabrielle.

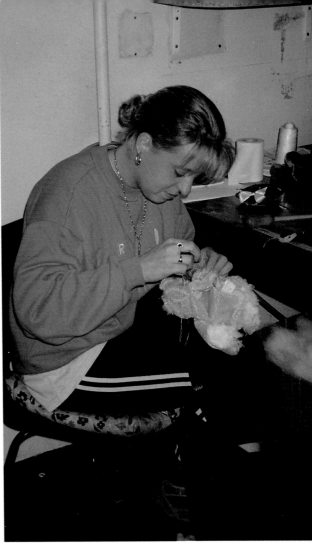

Hand stitching on a Pooh at Gabrielle.

Hand stuffing Pooh at Gabrielle.

Chapter IV
The Friends of Beatrix Potter

The Tailor, the Mice, and That Darn Cat

Much has been written about Beatrix Potter and her prolific writing and drawing. Certainly no other author/artist has captured so many animals with quite the detail and charm as she managed to do. Her life story whet the appetite of many biographers, with a tale filled not only with pathos but personal fulfillment.

If one wanted to chronicle the nearly one hundred years of products that have been marketed based on her drawings, it would fill a book and probably still not be complete. I personally know of three private collections that are immense in range and diversity. Magnify that by the hundreds who belong to the Beatrix Potter Society and you begin to realize the scope. Therefore, my effort is designed to show a *portion* of what has been available with the main focus on the book I find the most interesting, *The Tailor of Gloucester.*

The true tale began in the mid-1890s when John Prichard, a tailor in Gloucester, had a shop on College Court. One weekend he left an important article of clothing uncompleted and was astounded to find the garment finished when he returned to the shop on Monday morning. Finished, that is, except for one buttonhole. Prichard placed the waistcoat in the shop window with a sign beckoning everyone to patronize his establishment where waistcoats were made at night by fairies. He later learned the work had been done by his two assistants, but by this time the incident was a legend.

Beatrix Potter built upon this lore and changed the assistants from people to mice. In her version the tailor first ran out of buttonhole twist and then was too ill to complete the waistcoat that had been commissioned by the mayor. The tailor then entrusted his cat, Simpkin, to purchase a new spool of twist. While Simpkin was on the errand the tailor heard tapping and discovered the cat had been hoarding future mice meals by hiding them under teacups. The mice were released and, in gratitude, they finished the waistcoat while the tailor slept … except for one buttonhole. On this they left a teeny note that said "no more twist."

Potter was able to use the real shop in Gloucester as a model and, in her penchant for perfection, drew a rendition of a glorious waistcoat that was displayed in the South Kensington Museum. The first version of the book was written in a notebook complete with watercolor sketches. This original manuscript is now in the Philadelphia Free Library (a gift from Mrs. William Elkins). The exercise book included a letter to Freda Moore that explained it was a new story especially for the child because she had been ill. Beatrix told her that the tale was true, at least about the tailor, the waistcoat, and "No more twist!"

Portrait of Beatrix as a young woman.

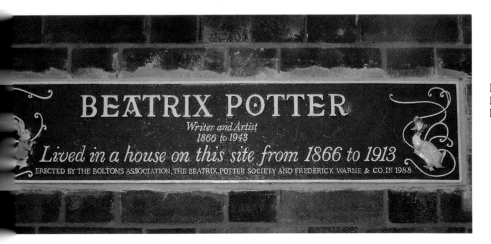

Beatrix Potter's birth site. The house in Bolton gardens where Beatrix was born is no longer standing.

The Life of Beatrix Potter

The birth announcement for Helen Beatrix Potter appeared in the London *Times* on Monday July 30, 1866:

> *"On Saturday, the 28th inst. at 2 Bolton-Gardens, South Kensington, the wife of Rupert Potter esq. Barrister-at-law, of a daughter."*

It seems such a small inauspicious line to announce the arrival of a woman who became a giant in children's literature. That course was navigated far in the future, but all her life and long before anything bearing her name materialized in print, she wrote and sketched.

Beatrix came by her artistic talents via genes and early exposure to art in many forms. Her grandfather was a textile designer and her father was not only a patron of the arts, but an accomplished painter as well. Rupert Potter entered the bar when he was twenty-five and married Helen Leech in 1863 at the age of 31. The Bolton Gardens house, mentioned as Beatrix's birthplace, was home to the family for nearly fifty years. The law is a finely structured occupation and requires such deep thought and dry reading material that surely Rupert found an exhilarating sense of freedom in wielding a paint brush. Most of his leisure time was spent visiting the Royal Academy and art galleries and, as soon as his daughter reached the age of reason, she accompanied him.

Beatrix, through her father's teaching, soon developed a discerning eye for what was good and, in her diary, critiqued what she had seen, often to the detriment of some famous talents. These sojourns with her father must have been a welcome relief to the tedium of her everyday life. As was typical in those times, she spent all of her childhood in the third-floor nursery, looked after almost exclusively by her nanny. She was brought down only to say goodnight and for special events. It was on rare occasions that her mother climbed the stairs to pay a visit. This probably suited the child, for she was slightly afraid of this maternal parent. For the following forty-seven years of her life, the third floor was Beatrix's playroom, schoolroom, and eventually her studio.

When she was six, a baby brother was born named Walter Bertram. Both children were called by their second names and to family and close friends simply *B* and *Bertie*. Beatrix was a delicate youngster, often ill, and understandably lonely because her parents discouraged friendships. Not only were they fearful of germs but, in their pompous way, "bad influences" as well. There were too many years between the siblings for them to be much company for one another, still it must have been a treat for big sister to have even a toddler around. She missed having friends, but at least her father spent time with her, encouraged other interests, and often discussed politics. What a strange introspective life for a growing girl.

Beatrix Potter doll: 12 inches including stand; beautifully detailed rendition of Beatrix as a young girl holding a rabbit by the late English artist Ann Parker; early 1980s. $400. (*Beth Savino collection*)

The Beatrix Potter Society was founded in 1980 by people involved in the curatorship of Potter material. The patron is Margaret Lane, Countess of Huntingdon, and the presidency is held by Bryan Forbes. The society holds regular talks and London meetings. An annual Linder Memorial lecture is given and a biennial study conference takes place in the Lake District and Scotland. The society, a registered charity, has a worldwide membership with offices in the United States, Canada, and Australia. A quarterly newsletter is sent to members and the group has an active publishing program. The subscription rate for an individual is $25 US dollars; $27.50 Canadian, and $30 Australian. Applications and subscription forms can be sent to: The Membership Secretary, Heatherdene, 30 Alpha Road, CHOBHAM, Walking Surrey, GU248NF, England.

Beatrix Potter (1866-1943) with Kep, the sheep-dog, at Near Sawrey

The saving grace were the wonderful and often prolonged vacations the family took. Her grandfather, Edmund Potter, retired in 1866 and moved to Camfield Place in Hatfield, Hertforshire (now the home of novelist Barbara Cartland). Beatrix adored it and (fortunately for her) visited often. The Potters also spent two weeks at seaside hotels every April. The entire summer seasons from 1871 to 1881 were passed at Dalguise House near Dunkeld in Scotland. It was here that Beatrix discovered her lifelong interest in wildlife. In 1882, the first momentous visit to the Lake Country occurred, now so closely associated with her that it might be considered Beatrix Potter Country. Her family spent from mid-July to the end of October in a large house called Wray Castle in Windemere.

Nearly all of her nursery life was put into drawing, having begun art lessons from a Miss Cameron when she was twelve. From 1881 to 1897, she wrote her daily thoughts and happenings in a journal. To insure privacy, she wrote in code. The code was so complex that it was thought to be indecipherable until it was finally broken in 1958. In later years Beatrix couldn't read it herself. Leslie Linder, a Potter specialist, tried for several years to break it and began to think it would remain unsolved forever. However, on Easter Monday, 1958 he discovered a clue and, with rising excitement, worked until midnight. At long last, nearly all of the code alphabet was exposed. Linder said that as he worked through the journal, page by page, he forgot that he was reading about the famous author whom he had revered for so long. Instead he found himself more conscious of getting to know simply a charming woman named Miss Potter. Leslie and his sister, Enid, ultimately left their entire collection of more than two-thousand pieces of Potter memorabilia to the Victoria and Albert Museum. The collection has since been moved to the Lake Country.

Wherever she lived, whether at home or on holiday, Beatrix made friends and found delight in warm and living animals. She was very attached to a pet dormouse, *Xarifa*, who was immortalized forty years later in *The Fairy Caravan.* Rabbits were especially interesting to her and her sketchbooks were full of them. She once bought a rabbit named Benjamin Bouncer, carried him home in a paper bag, and sneaked him into the nursery. He proved to be very tractable since he walked on a leash and was an exemplary model. Another bunny was a Belgian species, whom she named Peter Piper (she certainly had a penchant for alliteration). Beatrix worked ceaselessly to teach him tricks, which he would perform for food. His repertoire included jumping over a stick, through a hoop (both forward and backwards), ringing a bell, and, most amazingly, drumming on a tambourine. She drew Peter from every conceivable angle. Her love of drawing animals extended to her neighbor's pets as well. One household had guinea pigs and the sketches of them appeared in *Cecily Parsley's Nursery Rhymes* thirty years later.

When Bertram was eleven he was sent to boarding school, her governess left, and at age sixteen Beatrix was alone in the big house with just her parents. This rather pleased her for now she could concentrate on her painting, which had taken over more and more of her time. However, much to her dismay, her mother hired a new governess named Anne Carter. Anne turned out to be a warm and lovely person who became as much a friend as teacher. Years later her offspring played an enormous role in Beatrix's personal and professional life. In 1885, Anne left to get married and her pupil's education came to an end.

With her life unfolding into young adulthood and her schooling complete Beatrix began to think how nice it would be to gain independence by earning some pocket money. In 1890, she designed a Christmas card and sold it to Hildesheimer and Faulkner. The same year she sold illustrations to accompany a set of verses called *A Happy Pair* by Frederic Weatherly. Her working career had now begun, but as in most artistic endeavors the road to success was not always smooth. She submitted some sketches to the publisher Frederic Warne in 1891 who could see no use for them and they were returned. Her former governess, Anne Carter Moore, had several children by this time and Beatrix became attached to them and visited often. She also wrote letters to the youngsters whenever a visit was not convenient. The most famous epistle was addressed to Noel in which she related an illustrated story about Peter Rabbit and his siblings, Flopsy, Mopsy, and Cottontail.

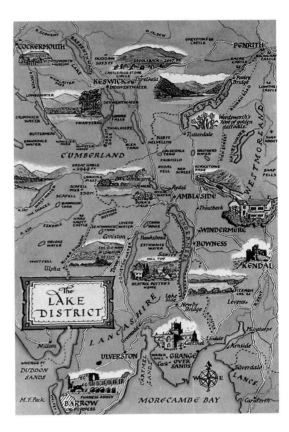

Postcard showing the Lake District and points of interest; produced by Salmon in England.

Seven years later she used this story (with an added center section to lengthen it) in a manuscript written in an exercise book. Black and white drawings faced each page and a colored illustration was used on the frontispiece. When it was returned by six publishers she decided to have it privately printed in an issue of two-hundred-and-fifty copies. Since the little book was ready on December 16, 1901 she gave them away as Christmas presents and sold the balance for "½ d" or half a pence each. Two weeks later they were nearly all sold out and two-hundred more were printed. She had previously consulted one of her friends, Canon Hardwicke Rawnsley, because he had regularly published sonnets. She hoped he would be of assistance in finding a publisher because he admired her works. The vicar was entranced with *Peter Rabbit* and once again the manuscript was submitted to Frederic Warne, who finally accepted it with the provision that all illustrations be colored. Two editions were issued; one in cloth and the other with paper boards. Beatrix Potter received £20 for her labors or approximately a penny a copy. The eight-thousand copies that were released on October 2, 1902 were all sold beforehand.

At the end of 1903, more than 50,000 copies of *Peter Rabbit* had been eagerly bought by the entranced public. Her royalties were beginning to mount and she asked to be paid monthly with two checks close together because she was preparing to buy some property in the Lake District. Her family had first visited the town of Sawrey in the summer of 1896 and Beatrix loved the countryside that was to become her home for the balance of her life.

With details of her extended writings in full bloom she visited the Warne offices frequently, becoming very friendly with Frederic Warne's unmarried son, Norman. He handled all of her office affairs and gave her the most support and encouragement. With such close contact and the same interests it was natural for them to become fond of each other. During the summer of 1905 he proposed, but her family deemed a man "in trade" unsuitable. However, Beatrix was thirty-nine years old and felt it was about time she became her own master and accepted the proposal. She wore an engagement ring, but no one beyond the immediate families were to be told.

In a sad twist of fate, just when Beatrix was on the verge of finding the companionship she so longed for, Norman became ill with pernicious anemia. He died on August 25, 1905 at the age of 37, just a few short weeks after Beatrix felt she could look forward to a lifelong commitment. Her devastation was even more acute since no one knew of her engagement and she was unable to find catharsis in talking about it. She had to hold her wrenching grief close and mourn silently and in private.

Beatrix Potter bought Hill Top Farm in the Lake Country with royalties and a small legacy. Hill Top was a working farm and she added more livestock, hired a caretaker, and added new additions to the house, as well. She eventually acquired other land holdings in Sawrey using the law firm of W. H. Heelis and Son to handle the purchases. Her affairs were looked after by William Heelis, and once again she found a romantic attachment. She wanted to become his wife, but once again her parents voiced objections, saying he wasn't good enough. They were seventy-three and eighty years old and expected their daughter to care for them and not have a life of her own. When they finally were brought around to accepting the inevitable, Beatrix and William were wed on October 14, 1913. The couple chose to live at one of her properties called Castle Cottage. Beatrix did not shirk her family duties and when her father died seven months later, she settled her mother in Sawrey with a companion.

In May of 1919, after many business reverses and a forgery charge, a new company, Frederic Warne and Co., was formed. They still retain the copyright to all Beatrix Potter products. The memorabilia based on her books became even more prolific than her writings. Years before she had even made a Peter Rabbit doll herself. It was fashioned of white velvet with whiskers pulled out of a paint brush and dressed in a coat and slippers. The rabbit was registered in the London patent office on December 28,1903.

Following her marriage, Mrs. Heelis put all her energies into farming and caring for the properties. In 1924, she acquired Troutbeck Park Farm. With all the duties necessitated by being a landowner, she lost interest in writing and drawing

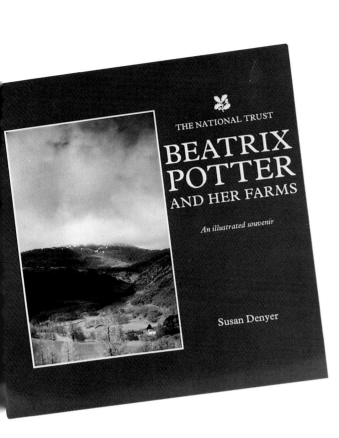

Beatrix Potter and Hilltop: An illustrated souvenir by Judy Taylor, published for the National Trust in England.

Beatrix Potter and Her Farms: A souvenir book by Susan Denyer, published for the National Trust in England.

Beatrix Potter and Hawkshead: An illustrated souvenir book by Judy Taylor published for the National Trust in England.

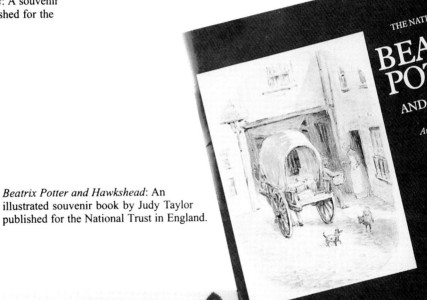

Village of Hawkshead.

for publication. Frederic Warne urged her to continue, but she resisted until finally doing *The Fairy Caravan*, not for him, but for David McKay in Boston. Warne was angered by this and threatened to revoke her copyright with his company. He didn't, of course, and she went so far as to do another book for the United States entitled *Sister Anne* with illustrations by Katherine Sturges. By then Beatrix was growing older, her eyesight was not clear enough for fine drawing and she felt simply written out.

After her mother's death in 1932, Beatrix answered letters, tended to her parents' house, and then returned to farming, an occupation she still strongly enjoyed. The many books she had written were still selling in the thousands, both in English and in the translations that included French, Dutch, Welsh, German, Italian, Spanish, Swedish, Norwegian, Danish, Afrikaans, Latin, Japanese, and Braille.

During World War II, one edition of *Peter Rabbit* was lost when a direct hit destroyed the printers. It was then agreed that all original drawings should be housed at Sawrey. Most of her fan mail came from America and her friends from across the sea also sent her food parcels.

In September of 1943, she contacted bronchitis, never fully recovered, and lost the battle for life three months later. Her death notice was recorded in a brief newspaper announcement:

> *"On Wed. Dec. 22, 1943 at Castle Cottage, Sawrey, near Ambleside, Helen Beatrix, dearly loved wife and only daughter of the late Rupert Potter. Cremation private. No mourning, no flowers and no letters please."*

The Queens Head, a Seventeenth Century inn in the village of Hawkshead in the Lake District; one of many historic landmarks in this lovely town.

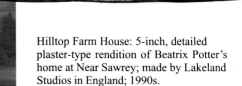

Hilltop Farm House: 5-inch, detailed plaster-type rendition of Beatrix Potter's home at Near Sawrey; made by Lakeland Studios in England; 1990s.

Pastoral landscape: A "Little Sawrey" view on a misty November day.

The Tales of Beatrix Potter

Even though the Warne edition of Peter Rabbit was so successful, Beatrix decided to privately publish her next book. She feared that Warne would not care for it or, at best, suggest changes she was not willing to do. Her five-hundred-copy edition of *The Tailor of Gloucester* was released in October 1902 and she sent a copy to him. Warne *did* like it, but was in somewhat of a quandary since Beatrix was coming up with ideas for books at a furious pace. However, after many discussions, he agreed to do two more—*The Tailor of Gloucester* and *The Tale of Squirrel Nutkin* were ready by Christmas of 1903 with deluxe editions bound in calico. They turned out to be just two of many, many titles.

For thirty years Beatrix's fertile mind and talented hands kept children supplied with delightful reading material. The small format was easily held in wee hands and collectors today find the petite books especially exquisite.

Determining whether a copy is a first edition is a formidable task. Because of the privately printed copies, different end papers and covers, as well as several printings in the same year, it is necessary to undertake a great deal of research. I find her books are high on the list of difficulty in positive dating as a first. I recommend a thorough study of Leslie Linder's 1971 book *A History of the Writings of Beatrix Potter,* published by F. Warne, before making a purchase.

Postcard with portrait of Mrs. William Heelis by Delmar Banner; available from the National Trust in England.

Privately printed editions of Peter Rabbit:
      First printing, 250 copies, Dec. 1901
      Second printing, 200 copies, Feb. 1902
Privately printed editions of The Tailor of Gloucester:
      Five-hundred copies, Dec. 1902
Peter Rabbit with plain leaf pattern end papers:
      First printing, 8,000 copies, Oct. 1902
      Second printing, 12,000 copies, Nov. 1902
      Third printing, 8,220 copies, Dec. 1902
      Fourth printing, 8,250 copies, Dec. 1903
Peter Rabbit editions with color pictorial end papers:
      Fifth printing, 10,000 copies, Oct. 1903
      Sixth printing, 10,000 copies, Dec. 1903
      Seventh printing, 10,000 copies, April 1904
      Eighth printing, 20,000 copies, Oct. 1904
First and early editions 1903-1931:
      The Tale of Squirrel Nutkin, 1903
      The Tailor of Gloucester, 1903 and 1904
      The Tale of Benjamin Bunny, 1904 and 1905
      The Tale of Two Bad Mice, 1904 and 1905
      The Tale of Mrs. Tiggy Winkle, 1905 and 1906
      The Pie and the Patty Pan, 1905, 1906, 1907
      The Tale of Mr. Jeremy Fisher, 1907 and 1907
      The Story of a Fierce Bad Rabbit, 1906
      The Story of Miss Moppet, 1906

The Tailor of Gloucester Shop at 9 College Court.

Another view of 9 College Court in Gloucester.

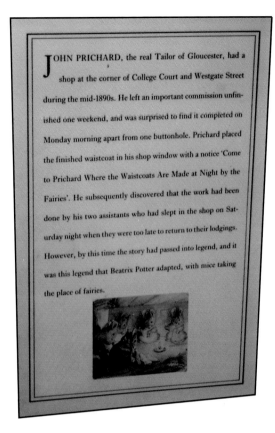

JOHN PRICHARD, the real Tailor of Gloucester, had a shop at the corner of College Court and Westgate Street during the mid-1890s. He left an important commission unfinished one weekend, and was surprised to find it completed on Monday morning apart from one buttonhole. Prichard placed the finished waistcoat in his shop window with a notice 'Come to Prichard Where the Waistcoats Are Made at Night by the Fairies'. He subsequently discovered that the work had been done by his two assistants who had slept in the shop on Saturday night when they were too late to return to their lodgings. However, by this time the story had passed into legend, and it was this legend that Beatrix Potter adapted, with mice taking the place of fairies.

The story behind the tale of the tailor framed and mounted at the historic house in Gloucester.

Pages from *The Tailor of Gloucester:* Original handwritten letter to Freda Moore from Beatrix Potter. Also included in the journal is the first written account of *The Tailor of Gloucester*. This journal is in the Rare Book Department of the Philadelphia Free Library. It also contains the first drawings. Dated Christmas, 1907. Shown is the letter and the first page.

The Tale of Tom Kitten, 1907
The Tale of Jemima Puddleduck, 1908
The Roly Poly Pudding, 1908 and 1913
The Tale of the Flopsy Bunnies, 1909
Ginger and Pickles, 1909 and 1910
The Tale of Mrs. Tittlemouse, 1910 and 1911
The Tale of Timmy Tiptoes, 1911 and 1912

The Tale of Mr. Tod, 1012 and 1913
The Tale of Pigling Bland, 1913 and 1914
Apple Dapplys Nursery Rhymes, 1917 and 1920
The Tale of Johnny Town Mouse, 1918, 1919, and 1920
Cecily Parsley's Nursery Rhymes, 1922, 1926, 1929
The Tale of Little Pig Robinson, 1930 and 1931

Miscellaneous books published by Warne:
Peter Rabbit's Painting Book, 1911
Tom Kitten's Painting Book, 1917
Jemima Puddleduck's Painting Book, 1925
Peter Rabbit's Almanac For 1929, 1928
The Fairy Caravan, 1952
Wag by Wall, 1944. 100 numbered editions
The Tale of the Faithful Dove, 1955. One hundred numbered editions and, in 1956, a regular printing.
The Tailor of Gloucester, 1968. A numbered edition of 1,500 printings from the original manuscript including a facsimile of the original manuscript.
The Tailor of Gloucester, 1968 and 1969. A total of 17,000 printings from the original manuscript.

American Editions:
The Fairy Caravan, 1929. David McKay
The Fairy Caravan. Limited edition of one hundred, David McKay
The Tale of Little Pig Robinson, 1930. David McKay
Sister Anne, 1932. David McKay
Wag By Wall, 1944. Horn Books Inc.

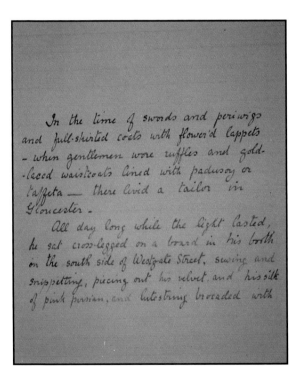

Second page of handwritten letter.

The illustration for the waistcoat; on view at the Tate Gallery;
©Frederic Warne & Co. Ltd., 1902.

A display showing Simpkin the cat busily hiding mice under cups in
the china cupboard, on view at the Gloucester Shop.

Waistcoat. The Tailor of Gloucester's waistcoat was faithfully
re-created in 1980 by the Gloucestershire Federation of Women's
Institutes. One of the members even cut up her wedding dress to
supply the satin on which the beautiful and meticulous embroidery
was worked.

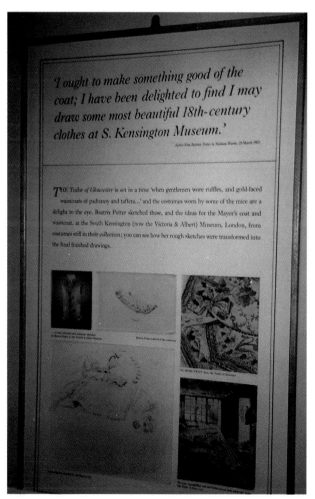

Beatrix Potter's reflections on the waistcoat. For the waistcoat she
drew from a beautiful example that was on display at the South
Kensington Museum (now the Victoria and Albert).

A spool of twist large enough to sit on at the Tailor of Gloucester Shop.

The kitchen at 9 College Court, Gloucester, in postcard format; ©F. Warne.

Postcard available at the Gloucester Shop of "Simpkin housekeeping;" ©1902. F. Warne.

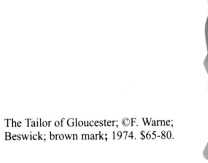

The Tailor of Gloucester; ©F. Warne; Beswick; brown mark; 1974. $65-80.

Lady Mouse from *The Tailor of Gloucester;* Beswick; ©F. Warne; gold mark; 1940s. $225.

Gentleman mouse figurine: 2.25 inches; the dressed mouse featured in the *Tailor of Gloucester;* made by Borders of Scotland. ©F. Warne; 1991. $50-60.

Simpkin figurine: 2.5 inches; the cat from the *Tailor of Gloucester* holds a cup and saucer; made by Borders of Scotland; ©F. Warne; l991. $50-60.

Crummles enamel box showing a street scene from *The Tailor of Gloucester;* the mouse and twist are shown on the inside of the lid; 1990s. ©The Berne Convention. $150.

The Tailor of Gloucester framed print: 4 inches square; ©F. Warne, 1993. $15-20.

Enamel box: 1.5 inches; *The Tailor of Gloucester;* made by Crummles, England; ©F. Warne; circa 1990. $125-150.

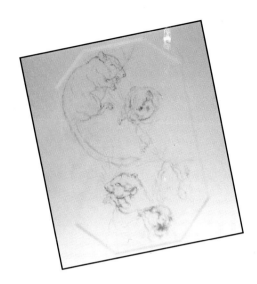

Drawing of the mice at the Gloucester Shop.

An enchanting mechanical display at the Gloucester shop re-enacts the mice busily sewing.

Book: *The Great Big Treasury of Beatrix Potter.* Contains nineteen stories and her original illustrations; ©1996 by Leopard, a division of Random House.

China dated from 1920 to 1950 is housed in the case along with new items for sale at the Gloucester Shop.

A sample of early Potter wallpaper at the Tailor of Gloucester shop.

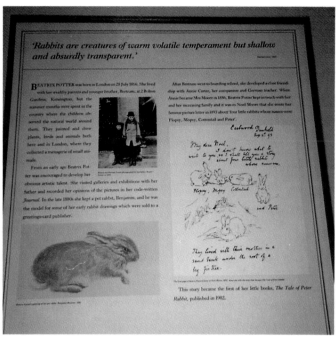

Sketches and reflections by Beatrix Potter, framed and displayed at the Tailor of Gloucester shop.

Potter memorabilia from 1920 to 1950 is housed in this case along with new items for sale at the Tailor of Gloucester shop.

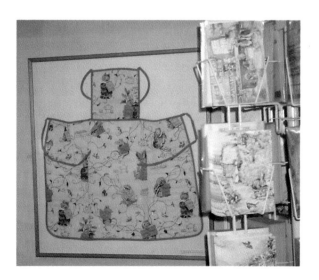

A 1923 child's apron made of fabric printed with Potter characters at the Tailor of Gloucester shop.

Doilies: 5.75 x 5.75 inches each; eight silk doilies painted by Beatrix Potter. They originally belonged to Alice Haydon (1863–1965) who lived in the Lake District. According to the family, they were painted and given to Alice by Beatrix; Anne Hobbs and Judy Taylor helped in cataloging them for Christie's, London, where they were sold in December 1996. (*Photos courtesy of Christie's, London*)

Illustrations of two doilies sold together from *The Tale of Benjamin Bunny* and *The Story of a Fierce Bad Rabbit;* ©1904 and 1906 by F. Warne. Approximately $6,600 for the two pieces.

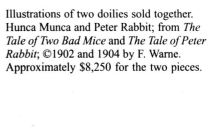

Illustrations of two doilies sold together. Hunca Munca and Peter Rabbit; from *The Tale of Two Bad Mice* and *The Tale of Peter Rabbit*; ©1902 and 1904 by F. Warne. Approximately $8,250 for the two pieces.

Illustrations of two doilies sold together. Jeremy Fisher and Tom Kitten from *The Tale of Jeremy Fisher* and *The Tale of Tom Kitten;* ©1906 and 1907 by F. Warne. Approximately $3,000 for the pair.

Illustrations of two doilies sold together. Mrs. Tiggy-Winkle and Timmy Tiptoes from *The Tale of Mrs. Tiggy Winkle* and *The Tale of Timmy Tiptoes*; ©1905 and 1911 by F. Warne. Sold for approximately $7,600 for the pair.

One cabinet showing a portion of the extensive Beatrix Potter collection owned. by Susan Wiley. (*Photo courtesy of Susan Wiley*)

Peter Rabbit tea set: semi-porcelain set consisting of a teapot, milk jug, sugar bowl, two cups, two saucers, and two plates; decorated in colors and gold after Beatrix Potter drawings; manufactured by Grimwades Ltd., England; circa 1920. ©F. Warne. $2,000-plus. (*Courtesy of Susan Wiley*)

Framed silk painting: 7.5 x 7 inches including frame; from *The Tale of Squirrel Nutkin*; after B. Potter's design; mounted, framed, and glazed; circa 1930. $155.

Framed silk painting: 7.5 x 7 inches including frame; from *The Tale of Squirrel Nutkin*; after B. Potter's design; mounted, framed, and glazed; circa 1930. $155.

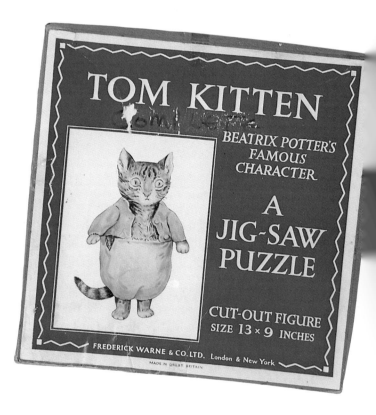

Jemima Puddle-Duck jigsaw puzzle: cut-out figure in original box; ©F. Warne; 1950s. $125.

Tom Kitten jigsaw puzzle: cut-out on cardboard; in original box; ©F. Warne; 1950s. $125.

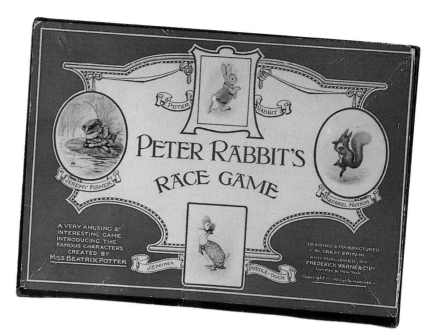

Peter Rabbit Muslin Game: unusual game printed on fabric; game pieces are cabbage leaves. No price available. (*Photo courtesy of Susan Wiley*)

Peter Rabbit's Race Game: 20 x 30 inches; large color pictorial board opens into four sections; includes dice, shaker, and four figures; in original box with all instructions; ©F. Warne; circa 1947. $425.

Game board for Peter Rabbit's Race Game.

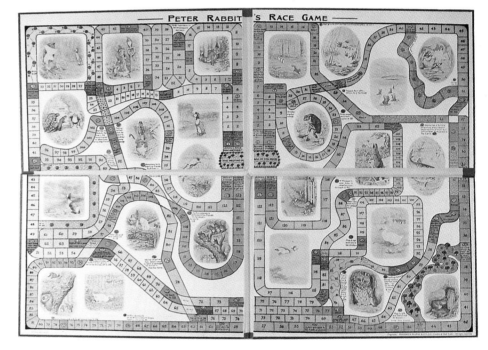

Figures from Peter Rabbit's Race Game: metal Peter, Jemima Puddle-Duck, Jeremy Fisher, and Squirrel Nutkin.

Peter Rabbit centennial edition: blue cloth box blocked in gilt and containing facsimiles of the stages in the publication of Peter Rabbit; ©F. Warne & Co., 1993. $425.

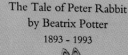

Centennial commemorative pamphlet

Video tapes: *The Tales of Beatrix Potter*; includes Peter Rabbit, Two Bad Mice, Tom Kitten, Jeremy Fisher, Benjamin Bunny, and Miss Moppet with eight rhymes by Cecily Parsley; illustrated and animated by Penny Yrigoyen and narrated by Sidney Walker; ©1986; distributed by Children's Video Library. *The Tale of Peter Rabbit and Benjamin Bunny*: a 1993, 100th anniversary collector's edition, ©1993 by ©F. Warne & Co. and Good Times Home Video.

Centennial contents: the privately printed book published in 1901; the letter, and an envelope addressed to Noel Moore.

Miss Moppet Print: 5.5 x 5.5 inches with frame; made in England; ©F. Warne, 1986. $15-20.

Silver disc pencil sharpener: 2.5 inches; Peter Rabbit is engraved on top; pencil is inserted on the side; made in England; ©F. Warne; circa 1990. $45-50.

Beatrix Potter stamp: Great Britain; 1979; the year of the child. $5-10.

Sterling commemorative coin: a one-crown money piece; souvenir of *The Tale of Peter Rabbit*; Gibraltar 1995; on the reverse is the Queen. $25.

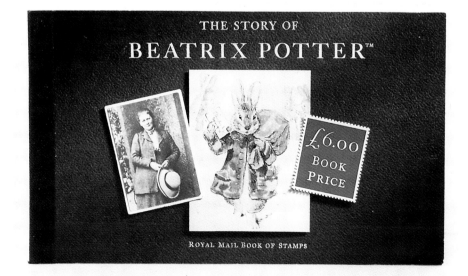

Beatrix Potter commemorative stamps issued in Great Britain for the centennial of Peter Rabbit in 1993. The English Post Office booklet contains regulation postage stamps as well as four new ones based on Potter's illustrations. Included are other non-postal stamps illustrating the characters and an outline of the author's life by Judy Taylor. The 300,000 copies were sold out in two weeks. $60.

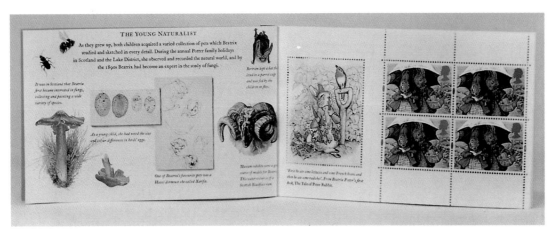

Stamps and data from the commemorative postal booklet.

Peter Rabbit: painted velvet; shoe-button eyes; felt coat and slippers; produced by Steiff from 1905 to about 1915; sizes from 4 to 14 inches. $2,000-plus. (*Sue Pearson collection/Photo courtesy of Michael Pearson*)

Beatrix Potter figure: 6 inches; handmade and painted; ©Gladys Boalt; 1987. $35.

Jemima Puddleduck: made by Steiff; circa 1926; jointed at the neck and legs. $2,000-plus. (*Photo courtesy of Susan Wiley*)

Beatrix Potter figure: 5 inches; handmade and painted; ©Gladys Boalt; 1987. $35.

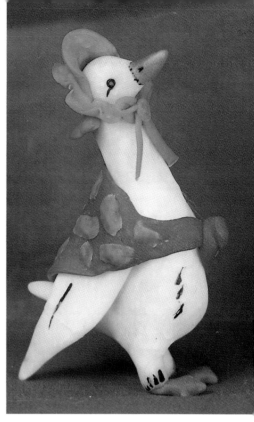

Beatrix Potter figure: 5.5 inches; Jeremy Fisher; ©Gladys Boalt; 1987. $35-45.

Jemima Puddleduck: resin molded by Vesna Sheffer, 1996. $25.

Tom Kitten: resin molded by artist Vesna Sheffer, 1996. $25.

Little Pig Robinson: resin molded by artist Vesna Sheffer, 1996. $25.

Peter Rabbit: 11.5 inches plus ears; plush with velour jacket and vinyl slippers; limited edition to celebrate the 100th anniversary of Peter Rabbit's first appearance in a letter to Noel Moore. The first book on the rabbit was published in 1901. Made by Eden Toys; ©F. Warne; 1996. $150.

Flopsy, Mopsy, and Cottontail: 3 inches long; from *The Tale of Peter Rabbit;* Beswick; ©F. Warne, 1954. $75-95.

Peter Rabbit and Benjamin Bunny: resin molded by artist Vesna Sheffer. 1997. $25 each.

Squirrel Nutkin: 3.5 inches; from *The Tale of Squirrel Nutkin;* Beswick; ©F. Warne; gold mark. $175-225.

Mrs. Rabbit: 4 inches; from *The Tale of Peter Rabbit;* made by Beswick a division of Royal Doulton; ©F. Warne, 1951. $95-125.

This enamel box was produced in a limited edition for the National Trust; 1980s; reproduced from a greeting card that Beatrix designed in 1890; ©F. Warne. $250-plus. (*Beth Savino collection*)

Tommy Brock: 3.5 inches; badger from *The Tale of Mr. Tod*; Beswick; ©F. Warne; 1955. $175-195.

Mr. Jeremy Fisher: 3 inches; from *The Tale of Jeremy Fisher;* gold mark; circa 1940; Beswick; ©F. Warne. $185-225.

Hunca Munca: 3 inches; mouse and babies from *The Tale of Two Bad Mice;* Beswick ©F. Warne. $195-250.

Jeremy Fisher: 3 inches; from *The Tale of Jeremy Fisher*; Beswick, ©F. Warne, 1950. $125-185.

Sir Isaac Newton: 3.75 inches; from *The Tale of Jeremy Fisher*; made by Beswick a division of Royal Doulton; ©1973; F. Warne & Co. $350-365.

Old Mr. Brown: 3 inches; from *The Tale of Squirrel Nutkin*; ©1963, F. Warne & Co.; Beswick Pottery. $100.

Old Mr. Brown: 3 inches; china figurine; Beswick; from *The Tale of Squirrel Nutkin*; ©F. Warne & Co. Ltd.; gold mark. $125.

Mrs. Tittlemouse: 3 inches; from *The Tale of Mrs. Tittlemouse*; Beswick; gold mark; circa 1940; ©F. Warne & Co. $175-225.

Pickles: 4.75 inches; dog from *Ginger and Pickles*; Beswick; ©F. Warne, 1973. $250-350.

Mr. Jackson: 2.75 inches; from *The Tale of Mrs. Tittlemouse*; Beswick; ©F. Warne, 1974. $65-75.

Base for displaying Beatrix Potter figurines. Shaped and colored like a tree trunk; marked "Beswick/Member of the Royal Doulton Group."

Foxy Whiskered Gentleman: 5 inches; from *The Tale of Jemima Puddleduck*; Beswick; ©F. Warne, 1954. $200-275.

On April 16, 1997, a major collection of Beatrix Potter memorabilia was sold at Christie's auction house in New York City. Doris Frohnsdorff had collected the outstanding works for thirty years and decided the time had come to part with them. The three-hundred-and-eleven lots included china, original drawings, autographed letters, first editions, and other ephemera. The following is a partial list of selected items with prices that include the buyers premium:

Book: *A Happy Pair;* by Frederic Weatherly; ill. Potter; 1890. $63,000.
Greeting card: ill. Potter; chromolithograph of two mice in a coconut shell; 1890. $2,530.
Book: *Our Dear Relations*; by Frederic Weatherly; ill. Potter; circa 1890 (only three copies known to exist.) $25,300.
Changing Relations; ill. Potter; circa 1894. $1,265.
Book: *Comical Customers*; ill. Potter and others; circa 1894. $3,220.
Book: *The Tale of Peter Rabbit*; privately Printed edition; 1901. $79,500.
Book: *The Tale of Peter Rabbit*. 1902. Second privately Printed edition. $23,000.
Books: *The Tale of Peter Rabbit*. Twelve other copies sold for prices ranging from $575 to $40,250.
Books: Over one hundred other titles published by Warne, in varying condition and rarity, were sold for prices from $115 to over $12,000.
This illustrates the difficulty in pricing her works and how important it is to make a thorough study of first editions before venturing into the marketplace.
Peter Rabbit's Bookshelf: A wooden shelf holding a complete set of the Rabbit books, circa 1934. $3,680.
Autographed letter: From Rupert Potter to Miss Moore. Oct. 17, 1910. $460.
Autographed letter: From Beatrix to Mrs. Martin. Oct. 28, 1913. $1,150.
Autographed letter: From Beatrix Potter to Dulcie. Oct. 18, 1918. (Includes small drawing of Hilltop farm.) $3,220.
Autographed letters: Other letters bearing her signature, (many with small illustrations,) realized prices from $460 to $5,750.
Potter Family Platter: Made by Minton with family crest. Mid Nineteen Century; paper label on back with a note. $575.
Photographs: A series of two-hundred, taken by her father, primarily of the Lake District and Scotland. 1879-1912. $5,750.
Victorian Scrap Album: Belonging to Beatrix. Inscribed by her "H. B. Potter From Mama/Valentines Day," 1872. $6,325.
Porringer and Milk Jug: Grimwade's Nursery Ware. circa 1930. $2,760.
Vienna Bronzes: Goody Tiptoes, Jeremy Fisher on lily pad, Tabitha Twitchet ,and three Peter Rabbits. 1930-1960s. $1,265.
Vienna Bronzes: Tom Kitten, Hunca Munca, two Benjamin Bunnies, Pigling Bland, Peter Rabbit, Mrs. Tiggy Winkle, and Fierce Bad Rabbit. 1930s-1960s. $2,990.
Vienna Bronzes: Twelve pieces. 1930s-1960s. $1,840.
Vienna Bronzes: Nine pieces. 1930s-1960s.$1,490.
Calendars, Records, and Posters. Forty-five pieces from 1974 to 1993. $1,035.
"Duchess with Flowers." Hand painted Beswick figure in original box accompanied by the book *The Pie and the Patty Pan*. Extremely rare. $4,370.
Biscuit Tin: Octagonal Peter Rabbit tin with lid and colored lithographed scenes; made by Huntley, Boorne, and Stevens for McVitie & Price, Edinburgh. 1939. $483.
Watercolor: 13.8 x 10 in. "The Three Witches of Birnam Wood." 1878 signed and dated in pencil. $11,500.
Watercolor: 8 .9 x 12.25 in. "Agaricus Xerampelinus" (mushrooms.) $13,800.
Watercolor: 11.5 x 8.9 in. "Fawe Park Garden" depicts a cat asleep in a garden; signed at lower left. Aug. 1903. $20,700.

For a more detailed and complete listing of items and prices see the Christie's New York catalog referred to as "Potter 7991."

Chapter V
Teddy Roosevelt, Seymour Eaton, and the Roosevelt Bears

Teddy and the Bear

It goes without saying that presidential memorabilia is most often sought by political collectors. That is true except for items relating to Theodore Roosevelt, the twenty-sixth president of the United States. Because of his affiliation with bruins, the Teddy Bear world is avid in their pursuit of his campaign mementos for without him there would be no Teddy Bear. All objects possessing his name or likeness are amassed, but particularly if it also contains a bear in any form.

In 1902, Mr. Roosevelt and his hunting party traveled to Mississippi to bag a few black bears. The president was not successful and, in an effort to aid him, his guides trapped a bear and offered it to Teddy to have a shot at. Of course, Roosevelt would have no part in such un-sportsman-like conduct. The episode was cartooned by Clifford Berryman in *The Washington Post* and entitled *"Drawing the Line in Mississippi."* This drawing ultimately became one of the most well-known cartoons in the world, giving Berryman a lasting place in bear history as well. Several stories abound as to how the teddy bear got it's name. One of Seymour Eaton's descendants (because of the Roosevelt Bear books) credits him with the naming. At any rate, we all agree that it is a direct result of the Berryman cartoon and certainly named after the president.

The list of items that feature Roosevelt's name or likeness is endless. Even those that include an ursine can be found with some regularity. However the enthusiasm for this charismatic man does not stop at collecting memorabilia. To walk where he walked and to see what he saw is all part of the interest. His birthplace in New York City, his inaugural site in Buffalo, his home on Long Island, and the Mississippi hunting grounds are all visited and enjoyed by his followers. Almost all recognized teddy bear artists, particularly Americans, have at one time used Teddy Roosevelt as the theme for some wonderful bears.

Drawing the Line in Mississippi: Cartoon by Clifford Berryman that appeared in *The Washington Post.*

David Worland and Brompton: Sign commemorating Roosevelt's famous bear expedition in Mississippi. (*Courtesy of David Worland*)

Vicksburg Museum: David Worland and his bear, visited the museum in Mississippi where a display of Roosevelt memorabilia is showcased. The bear in the showcase is said to have been a gift from Teddy Roosevelt to a young boy in 1907. (*Courtesy of David Worland*)

Framed Berryman collection showing a newspaper clipping in the center surrounded by original Clifford Berryman drawings; used as invitations and greeting cards over the course of several years. (*Barbara Baldwin collection*)

Seymour Eaton and the Roosevelt Bears

Frances Anne Ball, the only daughter in a family of eight, was born in Adair, Ireland, in 1827. She was named after her grandmother, Frances Long, who was the wife of her mother's father, John Piper. As a child Frances was friends with a young lad who not only bore the masculine spelling of her name but had entered the world during the same year. Their friendship came to a seeming end when Francis Eaton's family emigrated to Canada when he was fourteen. They were only the third family to settle in Euphrasia, Ontario. Destiny had a hand, however, in re-uniting the two comrades, for the Balls left Ireland six years later and settled in the same area of Canada.

Francis Eaton and Frances Ball were married in 1848, bought land near Epping, and raised eight sons and two daughters. Seymour Eaton, the fifth offspring, was born in Euphrasia Township, Grey County, in 1859. He was later to describe his large brood of siblings as a good-natured crowd with snap, brawn, and brains. The whole family had a sense of humor, as well, and Eaton excelled in this trait. He was also a bright child and his parents were determined to see that he received a good education. He attended State School #7, known as the Epping School, and then his father sent him to matriculate at Collingwood, a fete the man accomplished by skimping on his other money expenditures. After graduation, Seymour continued with his studies and in a year or two gained a teaching certificate. He taught for a period at Pickering College and a few years later he and John Lindsay, a native of the Griersville District, established Winnipeg College. Although this venture was successful, the establishment was disbanded after a few years.

On January 15, 1884, Seymour Eaton married Jennie Adair in Winnipeg, Manitoba, and eventually became the father of three boys and two girls. Two years after the wedding the young couple moved to Boston where Seymour accepted a teaching post. During the six years of this residency, Eaton became principal of Boston House College and originated a home study correspondence course. This form of education was the forerunner of the correspondence schools we know today.

The Eatons relocated to Lansdowne, Pennsylvania, a suburb of Philadelphia, which was to become Seymour's home for the rest of his life. In 1901, the couple built a tudor-revival house and called it Ath-Dara. I am sad to report that the large stone house is now an apartment building and no historical marker is in evidence.

In 1900, Eaton founded the Booklovers library that evolved into a circulating library and book club. This became so large that he ultimately created the Tabard Inn Library at 1030 Chestnut Street in Philadelphia, where books could be borrowed for five cents a copy. He was a prolific writer, working on several newspapers simultaneously and authoring a multitude of books. Charles Moose, who has made an intense study of Eaton, credits him with more than fifty books either written or edited by him.

His crowning achievement, however, was not his erudite works, but *The Tales of the Roosevelt Bears*, which were penned for children. Written in verse form and charmingly illustrated, they started as serials in twenty newspapers. They were so popular that Edward Stern, publishers, produced four books over a short span of years, and they were then divided into slimmer volumes by Barse and Hopkins. Eaton began the serials by using "Paul Piper" as a pen name, but reverted to his own name when the books were published. Piper was a family name that he borrowed from his great grandparents.

The four books were widely read, having gained inspiration from the most charismatic of all presidents, Theodore Roosevelt. In fact, his detracters accused Eaton of capitalizing on the president's popularity. I suspect they were envious of his success, but still this angered him for Roosevelt had expressed his delight, and Seymour, in his own words wrote of *himself* that he was a "lovable cuss with a reputation as a good loser and a reckless spender." Why would anyone want to malign such a fellow?

Teddy B and Teddy G were two bears who traveled the world, had many adventures, and even visited the White House. The volumes used four different artists for the drawings and color plates, but it is difficult to find much difference in execution. *The Roosevelt Bears: Their Travels and Adventures* was published in 1905 with V. Floyd Campbell as illustrator. *More About Teddy B and Teddy G: The Roosevelt Bears* in 1906 and *The Roosevelt Bears Abroad* in 1908 both utilized the talents of R. K. Culver. The final volume, *Teddy B and Teddy G: The Bear Detectives*, was illustrated in 1908 by Frances P. Wightman and William Sweeney.

The Roosevelt Bears inspired many products bearing their image. China, games, postcards, tip trays, jack knives, and lithographs are but a few of the many items collectors seek today. Many other products neatly circumvented copyright laws by making slight changes and referring to them by other names. They are still the Roosevelt Bears to collectors and coveted as well.

Seymour Eaton died on March 13, 1916 at the age of 58. Fortunately he lived long enough to see his creation skyrocket to worldwide success. I'm sure he would be pleased to know that the Roosevelt Bears live on in the minds and hearts of Teddy collectors.

Roosevelt campaign teddy: 4.5 inches; long napped plush; felt ears; bead eyes; gutta percha nose; cardboard pads; waxed thread claws; thought to be used as a Teddy Roosevelt giveaway campaign item; mint. Rare; circa 1904. $300 up.

THE RIGHT MAN IN THE RIGHT PLACE.

THEO. ROOSEVELT.
1900

Teddy Roosevelt kerchief: 24 inches square; white cotton with gun metal gray; Teddy as rough rider with political slogans; vice-presidential item; 1900; in modern frame. $600-650.

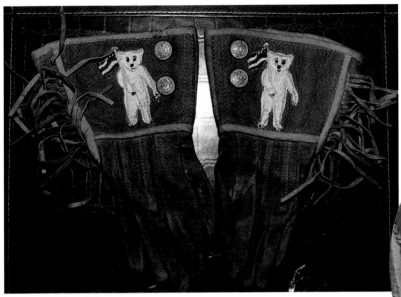

Rough Rider gauntlets: child-size; leather; unique; circa 1904. $500-600. (*David Worland collection*)

Cardboard coaster: 4 inches; Roosevelt wearing rough rider hat; colorful flag emblem; election of 1904 on the reverse side. Marked "Container Corp. of America." $15-20.

Framed Print approximately 27 inches; colorful hunting scene of Teddy Roosevelt; titled "President Roosevelt Bear Hunting;" marked "McLoughlin 1905." $195-200.

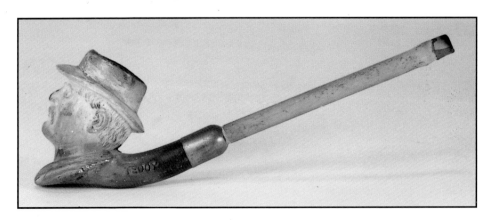

Theodore Roosevelt clay pipe with "Teddy" impressed on stem; rare; circa 1905. $195-plus.

132

Teddy Roosevelt postcard—an anti-Roosevelt campaign item; 1907. $40.

Teddy Roosevelt Campaign scarf dated 1912. $375-400.

Teddy Roosevelt campaign scarf with his face around the edge and his Rough Rider hat in the center; circa 1902. $360-375.

Roosevelt battle flag: 17 x 27 inches; National Progressive Party; 1912; red, white, and blue silk; especially nice since it features a bear. $550.

Teddy Roosevelt book: 1.75 x 2.24 inches:
unusually small book; cloth bound; profusely
illustrated; political item. $150-plus.

Right: Nicely matted
and framed Rough
Rider postcard, Teddy
"B" postcard, and
campaign button with
ribbon, all circa 1912.
$300-plus.

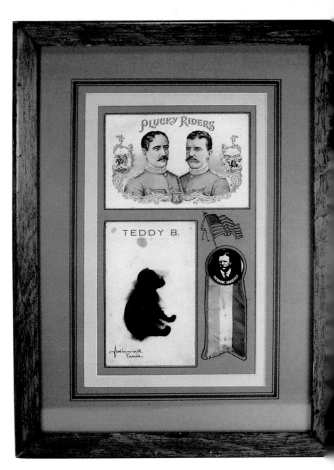

Tapestry table cover: 56 square inches: W. H. Taft in center; Teddy Roosevelt
as rough rider in all four corners; American; circa 1911; marked W. H. Taft.
$350-450.

Page from Puck magazine: 12.5 inches; cartoon dated April 10,
1912; titled "The New Tattooed Man: He makes an exhibition of
himself." Tattoos read, "Under no circumstances will I be a
candidate." Anti-campaign item; marked "Copyright 1912 by
Keppler & Schwarzmann." $75-95.

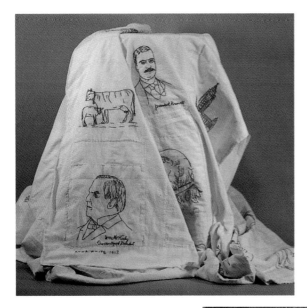

Quilt: 72 x 82 inches; red embroidered on white squares; subjects inspired by Buffalo, New York; Roosevelt (top right), McKinley, and various Pan Am exhibit biuldings as well as various other objects; interesting piece of Americana. Signed and dated 1914. $250-275.

T. Roosevelt, Roosevelt bear and teddy bear memorabilia. (*David Worland collection*)

Below: Teddy Roosevelt's rough rider uniform on display at Sagamore Hill.

Memorial day envelope dated May 30, 1929, with Roosevelt portrait and American Legion stamp on the front. $75.

THE MEMORIALS TO
THEODORE ROOSEVELT
in the village of
OYSTER BAY, N. Y.

FOUNTAIN
"In The Roosevelt Bird Sanctuary"
This Pamphlet is Issued Jointly by the
QUENTIN ROOSEVELT POST, No. 4
AMERICAN LEGION
and
THE BUSINESS MEN'S ASSOCIATION

MEMORIAL DAY, MAY 30, 1929

Roosevelt birthday button sold as a fundraiser for "Good Bears of the World" in October 1995. $5-7.

Postcard of Teddy Roosevelt and the Cracker Jack Bears; 1907. $30.

Left: Theodore Roosevelt Booklet: picturing memorials to Roosevelt at Oyster Bay, New York; issued jointly by the Quentin Roosevelt Post of the American Legion and the Business Men's Association on May 30, 1929. $75.

Teddy Roosevelt charm bracelet: gold tone with charms illuminating his career; from Sagamore Hill gift shop; circa 1955. $55-65.

A group of souvenirs availiable at the Sagamore Hill gift shop in 1992.

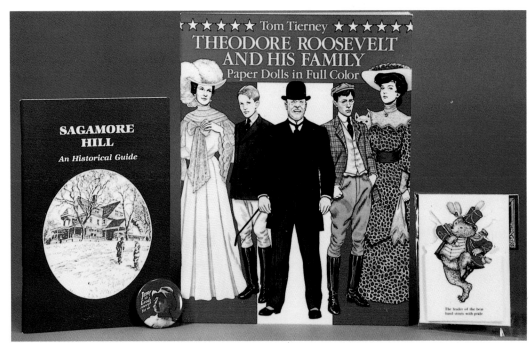

Teddy Roosevelt sand pail featuring Roosevelt riding a white teddy bear; circa 1907. $400-500. (*David Worland collection*)

Early 1900 card game made by The Teddy Bear Novelty Co; shown are a "Help" and cards numbered one through four depicting Roosevelt on a bear hunt; $350-plus if complete in box with instructions.

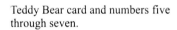

Teddy Bear card and numbers five through seven.

Cards eight and nine in which Teddy is victorious.

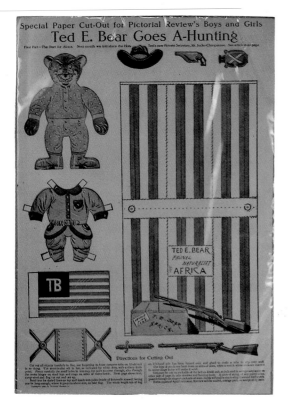

Paper cutout: Ted E. Bear Goes A-Hunting; *Pictorial Review;* 1909; Teddy with accessories and an African safari theme. $60-plus.

Teddy Roosevelt and the bear: 7 inches; painted muslin; non-removeable clothes; by Gladys Boalt; ©1993. $75.

Teddy Roosevelt doll: 8 inches; hard plastic with nicely detailed felt clothes; holds a Teddy Bear; made by Nisbet of England in 1983. $225-275.

Laughing teddy: 16 inches; 1995 Disney auction piece; one of a kind by artist Carol Stewart; entitled "Best Friends;" a 1995 Toby nominee; sold at auction for $3,000.

Laughing teddy: 4 inches; nylon velvet; fully jointed; open edition; 1995 Toby nominee; by artist Carol Stewart. $200 issue price.

Molded Teddy Roosevelt brooch: 5-inches; designed by artist Vesna Sheffer; clasp on back so it may be worn; 1996. Gift to author.

Teddy Roosevelt and the bear: 19 inches; wooden figure carved by folk artist Matt Cranmer; holding an all-jointed, 5-inch teddy made of fabric; limited edition of five; 1996. $500.

American Bear: 20-inches; original Rough Rider costume; circa 1907. $1,500-2,000.

Roosevelt laughing bear: 18 inches; gold mohair, glass eyes; mouth with two milk glass teeth opens and closes when stomach is pressed; Columbia Teddy Bear Company; circa 1907. $2,500-3,000.

Roosevelt laughing bear: 18 inches; coat wool; shoe-button eyes; red painted wooden mouth that opens and closes; four white teeth; probably made by Columbia Teddy Bear Company; circa 1906. $2,500-3,000.

Fabric doll: 13 inches; soft-stuffed Teddy Roosevelt; by C. Van Der Steur in 1979. $100. Caricature mohair cushion in the background resembles the Berryman cartoon bear; circa 1910. $200-plus. (*David Worland collection*)

This teddy resembles the Berryman cartoon bear. It is thought to be the example that was thrown from the presidential train on whistle stop tours. Googly Eye Ideal Teddy; 9 inches; circa 1904; shown with a limited edition Roosevelt statue and bear by Littlejohn; 1983. $2,000-plus. (*David Worland collection*)

Right: Artist Teddy Roosevelt bear: 18 inch, mohair face and hands; felt forms body and clothes; by artist Flora Mediate; 1980s. $225.

The 12-inch Steiff bear was given by Theodore Roosevelt to J. Alden Loring on return from their African trip in 1910. Clothes added by owner. Shown with Roosevelt memorabilia. (*David Worland collection*)

Artist Teddy Roosevelt bear: 15 inches; proto-type for Teddy in Rough Rider regalia by Beverly White; limited edition; 1990s. $500-550.

Artist bear: 14 inches; "T. R. Couldn't Shoot;" Rough Rider uniform; handcrafted replica rifle; distressed mohair; carries an all-jointed, 4-inch mohair teddy; limited. edition of 30; by Donna Hodges; 1996. No price available.

Seymour Eaton. Taken in 1902 at the age of 42. (*Photo courtesy of Charles Moose*)

The stone inscribed "Ath-Dara," the name Eaton gave his house in Lansdowne.

Left: Seymour Eaton's house in Lansdowne, Pennsylvania.

Entrance to the Tabard Inn, 1030 Chestnut Street, Philadelphia, Pennsylvania. (*Photo courtesy of Charles Moose*)

The Tabard Inn Corporation

The Consolidation of the Four Companies

THE BOOKLOVERS LIBRARY
THE LIBRARY PUBLISHING COMPANY
THE PHILADELPHIA BOOKSTORE COMPANY
THE TABARD INN COMPANY

Notice to Philadelphia Bookstore Company Shareholders

Notice is hereby given to all Shareholders of THE PHILADELPHIA
that by the *Agreement of Consolidation* between the four compan
BOOKSTORE COMPANY, THE BOOKLOVERS LIBRARY, THE LIBRARY
and THE TABARD INN COMPANY, approved and ratified by the Sha
companies concerned at meetings duly called and held for the pu
June 15th, 1904, and June 16th, 1904, respectively, the four comp
dated into a new company entitled **The Tabard Inn Corporat**
Department of State of the State of New Jersey, June 17th, 1904.

The capital of the new Corporation is $12,500,000; namely, $
Stock, 6 per cent. cumulative, and $7,000,000 Common Stock.
shares, both Preferred and Common, is Ten Dollars ($10).

By the terms of the *Agreement of Consolidation,* Shareholders i
BOOKSTORE COMPANY are to receive full paid and non-assessable
dated corporation at the rate of **two shares** of Preferred Stock and **on**
Stock for each share of stock in THE PHILADELPHIA BOOKSTORE
the said Shareholders respectively.

Shareholders in THE PHILADELPHIA BOOKSTORE COMPANY will
by the consolidated corporation in lieu of the usual monthly dividen
payable July 7th next, sums equal to the same, the said payments to
Shareholders respectively, on the said date, July 7th, 1904.

All shares of the stock of the consolidated corporation issued pu
of the Agreement are to be dated July 1st, 1904.

In accordance with the above, Shareholders of THE PHILADEL
COMPANY are hereby requested to send in their certificates of stoc
signed for exchange for certificates of stock in the new Corporation.
form of instructions should be filled out and sent to the undersigned al

All certificates should be sent by registered mail. The new
forwarded from this office will also be sent by registered mail.

JOHN E. B

PHILADELPHIA: 1323 Walnut St.
June 18th, 1904

The Tabard Inn notice of consolidation. Sent to Philadelphia Bookstore share- holders. (*Courtesy of Pat McCraw*)

The Tabard Inn Corporation

The Consolidation of the Four Companies

THE BOOKLOVERS LIBRARY
THE LIBRARY PUBLISHING COMPANY
THE PHILADELPHIA BOOKSTORE COMPANY
THE TABARD INN COMPANY

Notice to BOOKLOVERS LIBRARY Shareholders

Notice is hereby given to all Shareholders of THE BOOKLOVERS LIBRARY that by the
Agreement of Consolidation between the four companies, THE BOOKLOVERS LIBRARY, THE
LIBRARY PUBLISHING COMPANY, THE PHILADELPHIA BOOKSTORE COMPANY, and THE
TABARD INN COMPANY, approved and ratified by the Shareholders of the seve
companies concerned at meetings duly called and held for the purpose, June 14th, 190
June 15th, 1904, and June 16th, 1904, respectively, the four companies are now conso
dated into a new company entitled **The Tabard Inn Corporation**, registered in
Department of State of the State of New Jersey, June 17th, 1904.

The capital of the new Corporation is $12,500,000; namely, $5,500,000 of Pre
Stock, 6 per cent, cumulative, and $7,000,000 Common Stock. The par value
shares, both Preferred and Common, is Ten Dollars ($10).

By the terms of the *Agreement of Consolidation,* Shareholders in THE BOOK
LIBRARY are to receive full paid and non-assessable stock in the consolidated co
at the rate of **one and one-quarter shares** of Preferred Stock and **one and three-qua**
of Common Stock for each share of stock in THE BOOKLOVERS LIBRARY held
Shareholders respectively.

Shareholders in THE BOOKLOVERS LIBRARY are also to receive in li
annual dividend for the half-year dividend period ending June 30th, 1904,
held by them, **one-twentieth** of a share of Preferred Stock and **one-twentiet**
Common Stock in the consolidated corporation for every share of
BOOKLOVERS LIBRARY held by the said Shareholders, the same to be add
with the shares which the said Shareholders respectively would othe
virtue of the terms of the agreement.

All shares of the stock of the consolidated corporation issued pu
of the Agreement are to be dated July 1st, 1904.

Where by the terms of the Agreement fractions of shares in the consolidated
or Common, are payable to any Shareholders of THE BOOKLOVERS LIBRARY
stood to be of Preferred Stock so far as these fractions can be added together
fractions of shares over and above the unit shares so constituted shall re
consolidated corporation to the credit of the respective Shareholders concer
in any subsequent purchase of shares at their par value of Ten Dollars ($10

In accordance with the above, Shareholders of THE BOOKL
requested to send in their certificates of stock to the un
certificates of stock in the new Corporation. The accompan
should be filled out and sent to the undersigned also.

All certificates should be sent by registered mail.
forwarded from this office will also be sent by registered

PHILADELPHIA: 1323 Walnut St.
June 18th, 1904

The Tabard Inn notice of consolidation sent to Library Company shareholders. (*Courtesy of Pat McCraw*)

The Tabard Inn Corporation

The Consolidation of the Four Companies

THE BOOKLOVERS LIBRARY
THE LIBRARY PUBLISHING COMPANY
THE PHILADELPHIA BOOKSTORE COMPANY
THE TABARD INN COMPANY

Notice to LIBRARY PUBLISHING COMPANY Shareholders

Notice is hereby given to all Shareholders of THE LIBRARY PUBLISHING COMPANY that
by the *Agreement of Consolidation* between the four companies, THE LIBRARY PUBLISHING
COMPANY, THE BOOKLOVERS LIBRARY, THE PHILADELPHIA BOOKSTORE COMPANY, and
THE TABARD INN COMPANY, approved and ratified by the Shareholders of the several
companies concerned at meetings duly called and held for the purpose, June 14th, 1904,
June 15th, 1904, and June 16th, 1904, respectively, the four companies are now consoli-
dated into a new company entitled **The Tabard Inn Corporation**, registered in the
Department of State of the State of New Jersey, June 17th, 1904.

The capital of the new Corporation is $12,500,000; namely, $5,500,000 of Preferred
Stock, 6 per cent, cumulative, and $7,000,000 Common Stock. The par value of the
shares, both Preferred and Common, is Ten Dollars ($10).

By the terms of the *Agreement of Consolidation,* Shareholders in THE LIBRARY PUB-
LISHING COMPANY are to receive full paid and non-assessable stock in the consolidated
corporation at the following rates: The holders of Preferred Stock in THE LIBRARY PUB-
LISHING COMPANY held by the said Shareholders; and the holders of
LIBRARY PUBLISHING COMPANY held by the said Shareholders for each share of Preferred stock in THE
Common Stock **one-half share** of Common Stock for
each share of Common Stock in THE LIBRARY PUBLISHING COMPANY held by the said
Shareholders.

The holders of the shares of Preferred Stock in THE LIBRARY PUBLISHING COMPANY
shall also be paid in cash by the consolidated corporation a sum in lieu of dividends upon
the said Preferred Stock, at the rate of 6 per cent. per annum, from April 1st to July 1st,
1904, *pro rata*, the same to be paid July 15th, 1904.

All shares of the stock of the consolidated corporation issued pursuant to the terms
of the Agreement are to be dated July 1st, 1904.

Where by the terms of the Agreement fractions of shares in the consolidated corporation either Preferred
or Common, are payable to any Shareholders of THE LIBRARY PUBLISHING COMPANY the same shall be
understood to be of Preferred Stock so far as these fractions can be added together to form unit shares.
The fractions of shares over and above the unit shares so constituted shall remain on the books of the
consolidated corporation to the credit of the respective Shareholders concerned, to be taken into account
in any subsequent purchase of shares at their par value of Ten Dollars ($10) a share.

In accordance with the above, Shareholders of THE LIBRARY PUBLISHING COMPANY
are hereby requested to send in their certificates of stock to the undersigned for
exchange for certificates of stock in the new Corporation. The accompanying form of
instructions should be filled out and sent to the undersigned also.

All certificates should be sent by registered mail. The new certificates when
forwarded from this office will also be sent by registered mail.

JOHN E. BRYANT,
Treasurer.

PHILADELPHIA
June 18th, 1904

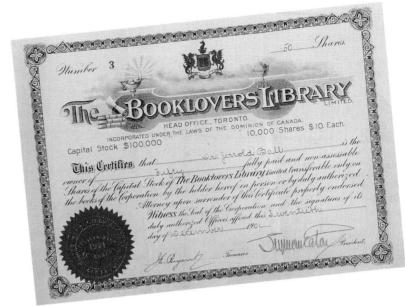

Capital Stock for the Booklovers
Library. (*Courtesy of Pat McCraw*)

Stock certificate for the Booklovers
Library. (*Courtesy of Pat McCraw*)

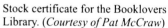

The Charterhouse Company capital
stock worth $50,000. (*Courtesy of Pat
McCraw*)

Ten shares of capital stock.
(*Courtesy of Pat McCraw*)

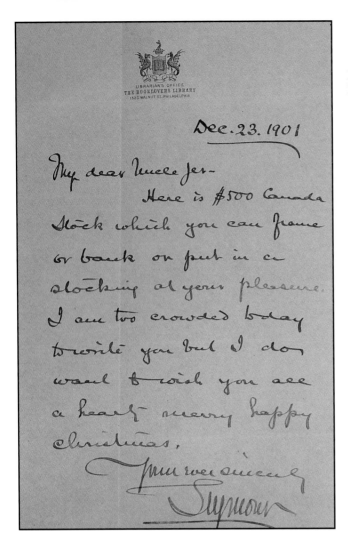

Dec. 23. 1901

My dear Uncle Jer —
Here is $500 Canada
Stock which you can frame
or bank or put in a
stocking at your pleasure.
I am too crowded today
to write you but I do
want to wish you all
a hearty merry happy
Christmas.

Yours ever sincerely
Seymour

Letter from Eaton to his Uncle Jer; dated
December 23, 1901. (*Courtesy of Pat McCraw*)

Prince Domino and Muffles: book written by
Seymour Eaton. Illustrated by C. Twelvetrees. A bear
also appears. (*Photo courtesy of Charles Moose*)

Books written or edited by Seymour Eaton. (*Photo
courtesy of Charles Moose*)

The Four Roosevelt Bear Books
by Seymour Eaton; published by
Edward Stern and Co; illustrated
in order of publication; ©1905
and 1906; ©1906; ©1908;
©1908 and 1909; *The Bear
Detectives* is the hardest to find
and the costliest to purchase.
$250-600.

Illustration from *More About the Roosevelt Bears:* Teddy B and G visit Washington and meet President Roosevelt.

Below: Postcard No. 9: The Roosevelt Bears in the Department Store. Souvenir of Philadelphia Industrial Exposition; circa 1907. $45.

Postcard No. 1: The Roosevelt Bears at Home. $40.

Right: Postcard No. 21: The Roosevelt Bears as Cadets. $40.

Postcard No. 20: The Roosevelt Bears at West Point. $40.

No. 20. The Roosevelt Bears at West Point.
" They joined a band with drum and flute,
With soldier hat and soldier suit."

" MORE ABOUT THE ROOSEVELT BEARS."
The new Teddy Bear Book for 1907, published September 1st.
Now ready at SMITH BROS., Oakland, Cal.
(This picture is one-quarter size of those in the book.)

No. 6. The Roosevelt Bears at the County Fair
" They walked on ropes drawn good and tight
And jumped through hoops and landed right."

Postcard No. 6: The Roosevelt Bears at the County Fair. $30.

No. 7. The Roosevelt Bears Leaving the Balloon
" They slid down ropes and hit the ground
And landed in Chicago safe and sound."

Left: Postcard No. 7: The Roosevelt Bears Leaving the Balloon. $40.

CUT OUT ON DOTTED LINES

TEDDY B.

PUT THIS BIB ON YOUR TEDDY BEAR

Right: Leather postcard with unusual design allowing for further use as a bib; 1907. $50-75.

Postcards Printed by Raphael Tuck; entitled "One in the Eye" and "The Cakewalk." 1908; series 118. $10-15 each.

Right: Framed postcards: 12.5 x 16.5 inches; professionally framed and double matted; circa 1908. $125-plus.

Print: 13.75 x 15.75 inches including frame. Print removed from Roosevelt Bear book and attractively displayed in oak frame of the period; circa 1908. $95-plus.

The Roosevelt Bears Go Swimming: 2 inches; made of clay composition with jointed limbs; one of a series designed by April Whitcomb Gustafson and distributed by Schmid in 1992; presentation box shaped like a steamer trunk. $50-plus. (*April Whitcomb Gustafson collection*)

These are the first factory samples of April W. Gustafson's conception. Notice the precise detailing of fish, creels, and costumes. The Roosevelt Bears Go Fishing: 2.75 inches. $60-plus. (*April Whitcomb Gustafson collection*)

The Roosevelt Bears at West Point: 2 inches; one of the series made in 1993. $60-plus. (*April Whitcomb Gustafson collection*)

Below: The Roosevelt Bears Travel the World: 2 inches; another in the series of April's work; 1993. $60-plus. (*April Whitcomb Gustafson collection*)

Left: The Roosevelt Bears Visit the Liberty Bell: 2 inches; 1993 series. $60-plus. (*April Whitcomb Gustafson collection*)

Below: The Roosevelt Bear Firefighters: 2.75 inches; the first factory samples sent to April for approval. $60-plus. (*April Whitcomb Gustafson collection*)

The Roosevelt Bears Visit the Circus: 2 inches; 1993 series. $60-plus. (*April Whitcomb Gustafson collection*)

The Roosevelt Bears Do the Cakewalk: 2 inches; 1994 series; advance sample set. $60-plus. (*April Whitcomb Gustafson collection*)

The Roosevelt Bears Play Baseball: 2 inches; 1993 series. $60-plus. (*April Whitcomb Gustafson collection*)

The Roosevelt Bears as Indian Braves: 2 in 1994 series. $60-plus. (*April Whitcomb Gustafson collection*)

The Roosevelt Bears Visit Central Park: 2 inches; 1994 series; advance sample set. $60-plus. (*April Whitcomb Gustafson collection*)

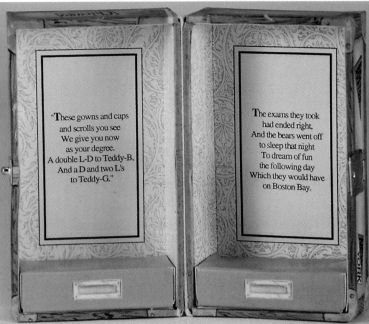

Each trunk in the series has the verse Printed as they appear in the books. Representative shown is from the graduation pair. (*April Whitcomb Gustafson collection*)

The Roosevelt Bears Graduate; 2 inches; 1994 series; advance sample set. $60-plus. (*April Whitcomb Gustafson collection*)

Roosevelt Bear pitcher: 5 inches; Buffalo pottery; scene of balloon descent; circa 1907. $400. (*Barbara Baldwin collection*)

Baby feeding dish: 9 inches diameter; marked on back "Royal lady Plate/ U.S. Feb. 7, 1906/Germany, Great Britain, France, Canada." $300. (*Barbara Baldwin collection*)

Cereal bowl: 5.5 inches diameter; heavy china bowl; scenes from the Roosevelt Bears on outside and inside; marked Buffalo China, 1912. $125.

Fabric bear: 16 x 17 inches; uncut; to be sewn at home; circa 1907; possibly one of a set of two; marked "Selchow & Righter New York." $495.

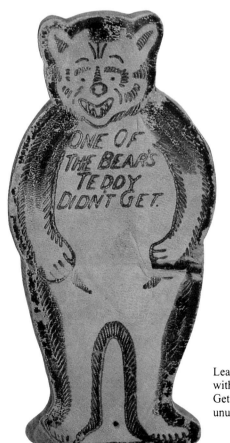

Leather pen wiper: 6 inches; figural bear with legend "One of the Bears Teddy Didn't Get." Felt pen wipers under the leather; unused; early 1900s. $225-plus.

Chapter VI
By Golly!

Florence Upton's residence at 2 Smith Square, London.

Florence K. Upton was born February 22, 1873 in Flushing, New York. Her parents, Bertha and Thomas Upton, had emigrated from Hampstead, a fashionable London area locale. In 1893, four years after her father's death, the family returned to England and it was here that Florence and her mother collaborated on the first Golliwogg book. Inspiration came when she resurrected a blackamoor rag doll that she had left behind on a visit to her grandmother years before.

The Golliwogg was no ordinary toy. As depicted in the thirty-one color paintings by Florence, he had a mischievous yet appealing appearance and became a beloved figure to thousands of children. Bertha wrote poems to tell the story of Golly, a hero who invented new exploits and, in spite of setbacks, usually succeeded. He was accompanied by two Dutch dolls, sometimes referred to as penny wooden. They came undressed so it was deemed necessary to outfit them for *The Adventures of Two Dutch Dolls*, published in 1895. The simple dresses were fashioned by cutting up an American flag (a practice not frowned upon in those days). Peg was garbed in red and white stripes and Sarah in the blue with white stars.

Florence signed her first contract with Longman's Green & Co. on the ninth day of October in 1894 when she was just twenty-one years old. She received a £50 advance and ten percent royalties on the first five-thousand copies. The book was an instant hit and although Golly was not mentioned in the title, it was he who fascinated the public. By 1909, twelve other books were published with varying degrees of success and they all had Golly in the title.

The Adventures of Two Dutch Dolls, 1895
The Golliwogg's Bicycle Club, 1896
The Golliwogg at the Seaside, 1898
The Golliwogg in War, 1899
The Golliwogg's Polar Adventure, 1900
The Golliwogg's Auto-Go-Cart, 1901
The Golliwogg's Air-Ship, 1902
The Golliwogg's Circus, 1903
The Golliwogg in Holland, 1904
The Golliwogg's Fox Hunt, 1905
The Golliwogg's Desert Island, 1906
The Golliwogg's Christmas, 1907
The Golliwogg in the African Jungle, 1909

While writing the books, Florence continued with her painting career, primarily in portraiture. She lived at the house in Hampstead for three years before moving back to New York City to enroll in the Art Students League. Periods of time, thereafter, were spent studying and painting in France and Holland before returning to England and a studio on Cheyne Walk.

Florence never copyrighted the Golliwogg and consequently others were free to capitalize on her genius. Shops were full of the dolls and a myriad of related products. Many of the Golliwoggs were handmade, but a goodly amount were manufactured by famous companies. Other writers borrowed the Golly as a protagonist in their own stories and nearly eleven-million non-Upton books have been sold. Even Robertson's, who have used his image as a logo for Golden Shred marmalade since 1910, avoided any reference to her name as the creator. The company even went so far as to announce that "Golly" was a mispronunciation of "Dolly" by backwoods American children.

The books and all that followed for over a hundred years are important. Still, this remarkable woman has not been credited for her role in the image of the black race in children's literature. I sincerely hope that my first book on the subject, *Enchanting Friends*, and this follow-up book will have some impact in setting that wrong to right. Even in England, where the books and dolls were once so revered, there are still uninformed people who think he constitutes a racial slur. At one point in time the Hampstead Library even shredded the books. Fortunately the word is getting out and countless companies and shops are featuring Golly in all his glory. Once again Golly reigns supreme.

In 1917, a full eight years after the last Golly book was published, Florence gifted a child she was painting a portrait of with a Golly doll. The little girl was enchanted and kept kissing him and calling him "a darling." How very gratified this artist was to know that her brainchild still was possessed of magic.

War clouds darkened Europe and in March of 1917, Florence donated the three dolls and 350 paintings of them to Christie's auction to help the war effort. The winning bid realized enough money to outfit an ambulance. Subsequently the prized items have been donated or loaned to public locations where they can be viewed and seen by devotees.

Florence Kate Upton had many friends and other interests during her lifetime. One of them was a fascination with the afterlife that included automatic writing. In this pursuit she allowed herself to become disassociated with her own will and let the spirits take hold of her mind and hand and write messages. In 1918, she automatically wrote that she would pass over to the world beyond in the year 1922.

The last twelve years of her life were spent at her studio and home on Great College Street in London. Florence's final days were spent in great pain and suffering following gall bladder surgery and her automatic writing proved prophetic for she drew a last breath on October 16, 1922. She was buried in Hampstead Cemetery in a plot that was completely covered with flowers and centered by a Golliwogg placed by a child who loved her. Her tombstone is inscribed:

> "*In Loving Remembrance of/Florence K Upton/of New York and Westminster./Who entered the Higher Life/Oct. 16, 1922 In His Gracious Keeping/of rare attainment as a Painter/She was possessed of a gift of Fantasy/and created the character of the Golliwogg/to the unfading delight of generations/of children.*"

Florence Upton's studio at 38 Cheyne Walk in the Chelsea section of London.

Florence Upton's final resting place.

Florence Upton's tombstone has toppled over and is flat on the ground. The inscription reads, "In Loving Remembrance of/Florence K. Upton/of New York and Westminster./who entered the Higher Life/Oct. 16 1922/In His Gracious Keeping./of rare attainment as a painter./She was possessed also of a gift of Fantasy/And created the character of the Golliwogg/ to the unfading delight of generations/of children.

Illustration of Golly, Peg, and Sarah Jane as it appears in the first book.

Advertising booklet: 7 x 9.5 inches; nine-page paper book used as advertising for Horne-Stewart Co., a Pittsburg, Pennsylvania, department store. This is a rare piece of particular interest, especially since it is not an English advertisement. The story inside, as well as the cover, are taken from the Upton book with no acknowledgement of permission; circa 1900. $225.

The Adventures of Two Dutch Dolls and a Golliwogg: A version that includes "Golliwogg" in the title; published by De Wolfe, Fiske & Co., Boston, rather than Longman's, Green and Co. of London. It is assumed that this was Printed circa 1900 when the original 1895 edition (that did not have "Golliwogg" in the title) proved so popular.

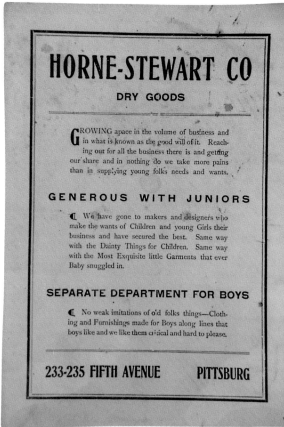

Back of the advertising booklet.

Book: *The Adventures of Two Dutch Dolls.* RePrint published in 1923; possibly a renewed interest after Upton's death; ©Longman's, Green & Co., London & New York. $225-plus.

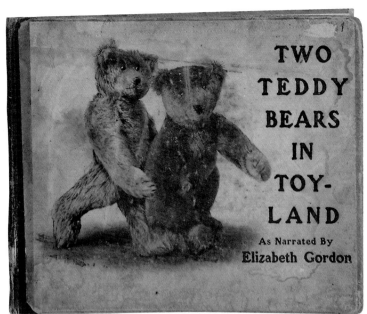

Book: *Two Teddy Bears in Toy-land*: By Elizabeth Gordon; photographed by Charles Wylie; Dodd Mead and Company 1907; told in verse form with teddies having adventures in Toyland; toys include a Golliwogg that emulates Florence Upton's original doll.

The Golliwogg at the Seaside: 5.25 x 8 inches; rePrint of a Golly book by Florence Upton; published by Longman's; 1960s; size is much smaller than originals, but still desirable and hard to find. $165-plus.

They did; and when the hostess came,
To see if all was right,
Imagine what her feelings were,
At seeing such a sight.

All her goodies were eaten up,
Poor Wolly on his face;
Dainties and dishes everywhere,
Scattered about the place.

Verse that accompanies illustration from *Two Teddy Bears in Toyland.*

Illustration from *Two Teddy Bears in Toyland.*

155

Illustration that clearly shows the resemblance to Upton's Golliwogg.

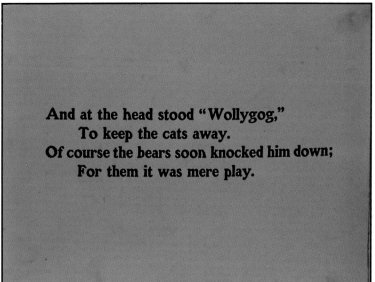

And at the head stood "Wollygog,"
To keep the cats away.
Of course the bears soon knocked him down;
For them it was mere play.

Verse from *Two Teddy Bears in Toy-land*. It's apparent that copyright laws were circumvented by calling the doll a Wollygog.

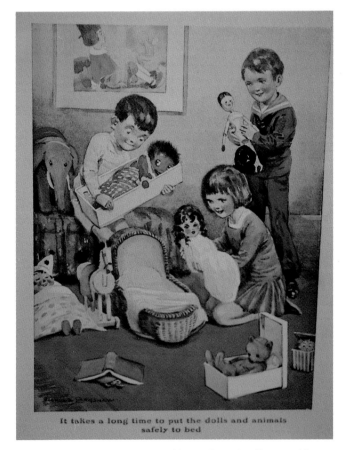

It takes a long time to put the dolls and animals safely to bed

Book: *The Cheery Chicks:* by Harold Earnshaw; Smallman and Ingram Ltd, London; contains six color and thirteen black and white and sepia-tone pages of pictures of children and their nursery toys; one page is shown in which a Golliwogg appears; early 1900s. $45-50. (*Terri Kovacs collection*)

Book: *The Golliwogg News* : Enchanting story of three children and a toy newspaper. By Phillip and Fay Inchfawn; published by S. W. Partridge and Co. Ltd., Old Bailey; black-and-white illustrations by T. C. Smith; 1913. $150-plus

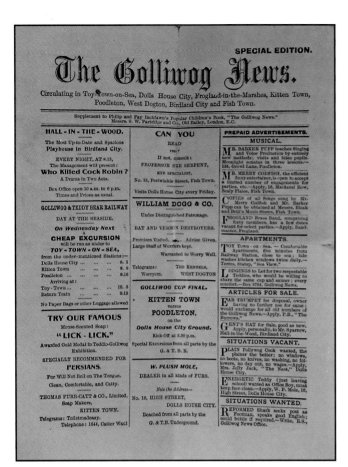

The Golliwogg News: a toy newspaper that is included in the book *The Golliwogg News*. Four pages of extremely amusing advertisements, want-ads and feature articles. 1913.

Book: *The Golliwogg News* by Fay and Phillip Inchfawn; published by Partridge; 1913. $150-plus. (*David Worland collection*)

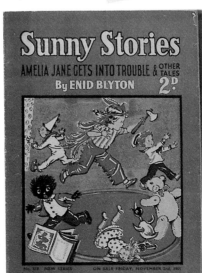

Book: *Bobo's Adventures:* 7.25 x 10.5 inches; produced and Printed in Great Britain; story of Bobo and his adventures with a Golliwogg, a teddy and other animals; sixteen pages in soft-cover format; circa 1920. $150. (*Terri Kovacs collection*)

Book: *Noddy Colour Strip Book*: By Enid Blyton; published by Sampson, Low Marston & Co. Ltd., London; further adventures with many characters including Golliwoggs; comic strip format; 1950s. $34-45.

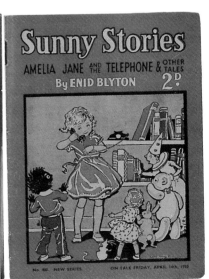

Sunny Stories: Two soft-cover books by Enid Blyton; a series that featured a Golliwogg; 1950s. $25 each.

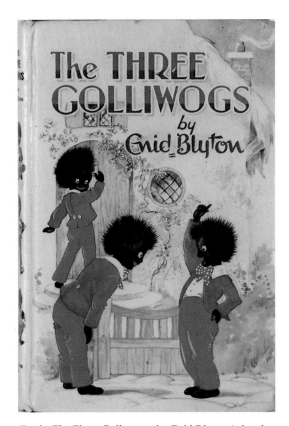

Book: *The Three Golliwoggs* by Enid Blyton (who also wrote the "Noddy" series). ©George Newness Ltd; published by Dean & Sons Ltd; 1969. $60.

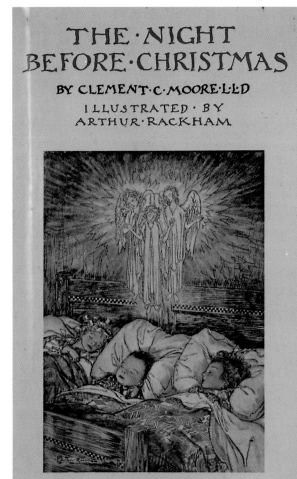

Book: *The Night Before Christmas*; 5.75 x 8.5 inches; illustrated by Arthur Rackman; 1976. $75. (*Terri Kovacs collection*)

Filled all the stockings

Page from the Rackham book showing Santa at work; illustration contains a Teddy, a Golly, and a Peg doll.

Robertson's Surprise Book: 1.5 x 7 inches; full color; filled with puzzles, games, and other amusements; circa 1960. $45-50. (*Terri Kovacs collection*)

The original Golliwogg and Dutch dolls that belonged to Florence Upton; on loan to the Bethnal Green Museum of Childhood. (*Photograph courtesy of the Victoria and Albert Museum, London*)

Steiff Golliwogg: 13 inches; felt with embroidered features and shoe-button eyes; leather shoes; all jointed; rare; circa 1910. $8,000-plus.

Golliwogg: 14 inches; circa 1900; all original; played with condition; leather on nose is mostly gone as well as sealskin hair; shown with photo of the doll when new; part of a collection that contained all thirteen of the books. $275.

Golliwoggs: 7.5 and 10.5 inches; handmade; fabric with shoe-button and pearl-button eyes; circa 1915. No price available. (*Richard Wright collection/Anne Jackson photograph*)

Far left: Handmade Golly: 17 inches; silk face with applied nose; button eyes; silk and wool clothes; circa 1915. $650.

Left: Golliwogg: 18 inches; velvet; shoe-button eyes backed by large linen buttons; all jointed; plush hair; British; circa 1920. Made by Chad Valley of England. $425-plus.

Below left: Felt Golly: 12 inches; pin-jointed legs; not jointed arms; fabric shoes; four pronged button in right ear; possibly German; circa 1915. $600. (*Becky Mucchetti collection*)

Below: British Golly: 18 inches; handmade; silk and sateen; embroidered features; circa 1920. $600.

Left: Handmade Golly: 20 inches; interesting colors and conception; cotton except for frayed silk hair; sewn on features; tie added; circa 1920. $400-plus. (*Becky Mucchetti collection*)

Right: British Golliwogg: 13 inches; cotton and felt; sealskin hair; circa 1935. $100.

Handmade Golly: 11 inches; twill face, hands and feet; linen button eyes; embroidered nose and mouth; cotton hair; velvet clothes; British; circa 1930. $300-plus.

Left: Made by Dean's Company of England. Golliwogg: 23 inches; all felt with plush hair and button eyes; circa 1935. $625.

Right: Made by Chad Valley of England. Golliwogg: 18 inches; all velvet including eyes; painted nostrils and mouth; tagged on foot. circa 1930. $550-plus.

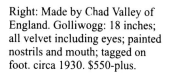

Left: Handmade British
Golliwogg: 29 inches; felt;
yarn hair; wool clothes; circa
1940. $425.

Right: Made by Pedigree of
Ireland. Golliwogg: 22 inches;
velvet with wool and corduroy
clothes; plastic eyes and
mouth; tagged on back of
neck; circa 1950. $275.

Golliwogg: 20 inches; British; handmade;
circa 1940. $165.

Left: Quaint Golly girl
and boy: 9 inches;
handmade; dressed in
felt and leather; unusual
gold hair color; British;
circa 1940. $500-plus.

Right: British
Merrythought
Golliwogg: 22 inches;
felt; glued-on eyes and
mouth; cotton clothes;
chimes in body; circa
1950; tag on foot. $225-
250.

Australian Joy Toy: 34 inches; cotton; roll-around eyes; felt mouth; redressed; circa 1950. $150-plus. (*Dot Gillett collection*)

Australian doll: 22 inches; cotton; Printed nose and mouth; plastic roll-around eyes; made by Joy Toys; 1950s. $115. (*Dot Gillett collection*)

Australian Golly: 24 inches; all cotton; felt mouth; roll-around eyes; made by Joy Toys; 1950s. $130-plus. (*Dot Gillett collection*)

Left: Australian Joy Toy: 34 inches; cotton top; corduroy pants; Printed face; 1950s. $150. (*Dot Gillett collection*)

Right: Australian Joy Toy: 21 inches; all cotton; disc eyes; foam filled; circa 1950. $112-plus. (*Dot Gillett collection*)

Left: Australian doll: 25 inches; celluloid face; plush top; corduroy bottom; colorful; probably made by Emil Toys; circa 1950. $150. (*Dot Gillett collection*)

Left: Australian Joy Toy Golly: 21 inches; all cotton; roll-around eyes; foam filled; felt nose and mouth; circa 1950. (*Dot Gillett collection*)

Right: Australian dolls: 12 and 16 inches; cotton and velvet; plastic eyes; made by Jakas Toys; 1950s. $93-108. (*Dot Gillett collection*)

Australian Gollys: 14, 15, and 15.5 inches; vinyl faces; cotton bodies and stuffing. The Golly on the left side and the one in the back have corduroy tops and hands; made by Joy Toys; 1950s. $112-150 each. (*Dot Gillett collection*)

Australian Golly: 17 inches; celluloid face; cotton trousers; velvet jacket; foam filled; circa 1950; made by Emil Toys. $185. (*Dot Gillett collection*)

British Golliwogg pajama case: 28 inches; made of linen with tin eyes; zipper in back to hold night clothes; maker unknown; circa 1950. $165-175.

Australian Golly: 16 inches; felt face; cotton pants; velvet hands and feet; this Golly is pictured in the December 24, 1958 magazine *Women's Weekly.* $112. (*Dot Gillett collection*)

Left: British Golliwogg: 16 inches; cotton; Printed made-on clothes; removeable jacket; plastic eyes; made by Dean's ; 1960s. $100-125.

Right: Merrythought Golliwogg: 14 inches; velvet and cotton; chimes ring when Golli is picked up; interesting because it retains Harrod's price tag; 1960s. $500. (*Maria Bluni collection*)

Below: British Golliwogg: 15 inches; cotton fabric; not jointed; 1960s. $80-100.

British Golliwogg: 16 inches; not jointed; felt and cotton; unusual hair; pasted-on features; commercially made; 1960s. $95-100.

Right: Merrythought Golliwogg: 12 inches; felt; label on foot; 1964–1966. $275-300. (*Maria Bluni collection*)

British Golliwogg: 32 inches; cotton and felt; soft stuffed; tagged "Pedigree;" circa 1960. $200-plus.

Golli-Girl: 18 inches; made in England by Wendy Boston; typical Boston features; a girl Golli is much harder to find; label on right foot; circa 1960. $450-plus.

Wendy Boston Golliwogg Girl: showing her padded rump that facilitates easy sitting.

Wendy Boston Golliwogg: 14 inches; cotton with plush hair; circa 1960. $95-120. British Golliwogg: 9 inches; cotton with plush hair; ethnic fabric dress. circa 1940. $75-90.

Handmade Golli: 36 inches; black felt; curly yarn hair; glitter fabric trousers; bowtie and trim; vinyl shoes; made in England; circa 1960. $400.

British Golliwogg: 25 inches; cotton; felt features glued on; commercially made; 1960s. $125.

Merrythought Golly and Bear: 17 inches; replicas of 1932 catalogue pieces. Teddy is all jointed; Golly is not jointed; mint-in-box condition; a John Axe design; 1989; signed by Oliver Holmes, director of Merrythought Co. Ltd.

Robertson Golli: 11.5 inches; felt doll made as a premium; circa 1960. $110. Chad Valley Golli: 16 inches; cotton and felt; circa 1960. $145.

Left: British Dean's Golliwogg: 14 inches; velvet, cotton, and felt; a re-issue of the company's traditional Golly; 1960s. $75-85.

Right: Australian Golly: 13 inches; same conception and conformation as earlier dolls made by Jakas Toys except fabric is now of nylon; 1995. $50-plus. (*Dot Gilleti collection*)

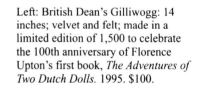

Below: Golliwogg: 13 inches; velour, cotton, and felt with pasted-on features and yarn hair; made in Australia; 1990s. Gift to author.

Left: British Dean's Gilliwogg: 14 inches; velvet and felt; made in a limited edition of 1,500 to celebrate the 100th anniversary of Florence Upton's first book, *The Adventures of Two Dutch Dolls.* 1995. $100.

Right: Steiff Golliwogg and Teddy: 4 and 9 inches; pair made for the 10th Festival of Steiff in 1995, sponsored by the Toy Store in Toledo, Ohio; "Golli G and Teddy B" limited edition of 1,500. $450-plus.

Molly Golly and Peg: 9 inches; made by Steiff for the Toy Store in Toledo; the first girl Golli this company has ever made; Molly is made of felt and Peg is wood with a cotton dress; introduced at the Steiff Festival in 1996. $225 issue price.

Scottish Golly: *Whoopsy*; 13 inches; made of cotton and wool; manufactured in the Outer Hebrides by the Harris Tweed Co; 1996. $200. (*Becky Mucchetti collection*)

Golliwoggs: 14 inches; 1996 prototypes; made with embroidered faces; Gabrielle Designs.

Far left: R. John Wright Golliwogg: 10 inches; molded felt; painted features; beautifully detailed felt clothes and leather shoes; the first item available to club members only; certificate and presentation box; numbered, limited edition of 2,500; 1996. $535 issue price, will probably double.

Left: Artist Golly: 8 inches; by British artist Vanessa Littleboy; not jointed; open edition; 1990s. $35-50. (*David Worland collection*)

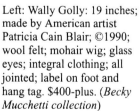

Left: Wally Golly: 19 inches; made by American artist Patricia Cain Blair; ©1990; wool felt; mohair wig; glass eyes; integral clothing; all jointed; label on foot and hang tag. $400-plus. (*Becky Mucchetti collection*)

Right: Steiff Jolly Golly and Teddy Bear; 13 and 12 inches; produced in 1996 in a limited edition of 1,500 pieces for Dolly Land in England. $650. (*Becky Mucchetti collection*)

Little Golliwoggs: 3 inches; Jubilee themes made for Kansas City show by artist Linda Davis in the 1990s. One is a finger puppet. $60-plus at issue. (*Courtesy of Linda Davis*)

Showing the Golly side of "Inseparable Friends." (See below)

Artist Golliwogg: 10 inches; wool felt; hand-painted face; segmented, poseable limbs; removeable vest; 1990s; one of a kind by artist Lin Van Houten. $150-plus.

"Golly's Inseparable Friend," Flip Flop Teddy: 14 inches; limited edition of 25; 1990s by artist Linda Davis. $200-plus. (*Courtesy of Linda Davis*)

Artist Gollies: made by Australian artist Romy Roeder; wool and other fabrics; all jointed; 1995. $135.

Artist Golly: 13 inches; by Australian artist Lexie Haworth; felt with mohair wig; all jointed; 1995; gift to owner. (*David Worland collection*)

Golly: 4 inches, made of velvet and ultra-suede; open edition; released in 1995; by Carol Stewart. $200-plus.

Artist Golliwoggs: Lil Wogette: 3 inches; ultra-suede; long braids; fully jointed; gold-leaf charm; finely detailed; 1995 open edition. Lil Wog: 3 inches; ultra-suede; hair stands on end; finely detailed; 1995; open edition. Both made by Randy Martin of Lil Brother's Bears. $150 each. (*Photo courtesy of Randy Martin*)

"Doo-See-Doo:" 3 inches; Western pair by artist Linda Davis for the Kansas Jubilee in 1995. $160 pair. (*Courtesy of Linda Davis*)

Left: Golly Gee and Bear: 12 and 6 inches; made by Ballard Baines Bear Co., 1995; charming and detailed; Golly has integral velour clothes; leather gloves; felt and cord details; Teddy is mohair; both are all jointed. $350. (*Becky Mucchetti collection*)

Artist Golli: 4.5 inches; mohair that is shaved on face and left long for hair; cotton and felt clothes form body; painted details; pellet-filled body; by Canadian artist Trudy Yelland; 1995; gift to author.

Below: Prototype Golly: 15.5 inches; Steiff look-a-like by artist Jeanette Warner; to celebrate 100 years of the Golliwogg in 1995; felt with removeable clothes; shown with Peg Dolls by Eric Horne of England. Bears also made by Jeanette. $250-plus.

Sailor Golly: all jointed; made by Australian artist Romy Roeder; 1996. $135.

Golli G: 13 inches; imaginative Golliwogg made by artist Carol Martin; 1995. $150-175.

Artist Golly: bellhop design by Australian artist Romy Roeder; all jointed; 1996. $135.

Jester Golly: clown style; fully jointed; by Australian artist Romy Roeder; 1996. $135.

Bathing Golly: vintage-style bathing garment forms the body of this Golly made by Australian artist Romy Roeder; 1996. $135.

Best Friends—Tea for Two: 8 and 19 inches; limited edition of 18 sets by artist Karen A. Meer in 1996; "Wolli Golly" is meticulously dressed in wool and upholstery velvet and trimmed in lace and gold; "Bert" is mohair and wears a top hat and a star trimmed bow; "Wolli's" top hat forms a table for the china tea set. $450-plus.

Sir Willowbee: 9 inches; Golly is made of ultra-suede; side-glancing glass eyes and recycled fox fur hair; 1996; by artist Terri Kovacs. $150.

Gylian: 15 inches; made of cashmere and ultra-suede with pasted-on features; non jointed; limited edition of five; 1996, by artist Linda Davis. $130. Artist Golliwoggs: 7 to 9 inches; a group of all-jointed Gollys by artist Linda Davis; cotton and felt with glass eyes; 1990s. $80-plus each. (*Courtesy of Linda Davis*)

Left: Golliwogg prototype: 15 inches; black felt; ultra-suede, made-on clothes; maribou hair; designed by the author for Gabrielle Designs Ltd., England; 1995. The finished issue sold for $140 in an edition of 500 pieces with certificate.

Right: Golliwogg: 13 inches; felt and cotton; black fox hair; all jointed; made by author in 1996. $200.

Left: Artist Golliwogg: 3.5 inches; ultra-suede and cotton; finely detailed; designed by artist Deb Canham and produced in the Orient; limited edition of 3,000; 1996. Gift to author.

Right: Golliwoggs: 14 and 11 inches; felt and ultrasuede leather; made-on ultrasuede clothes; designed by author; 1997. $175-250.

Golliwogg: 14 inches; designed by author; 1997; ultra leather face and boots; removeable sailor suit. $250.

Artist Celia Baham holds an original teddy bear. The bear is holding a teddy body with a Golliwogg head. The Teddy/Golly was inspired by a book featured in *Enchanting Friends*.

Left: Artist Golliwogg: 17 inches; made by author; one of a kind; ultra leather face; kid gloves and shoes; made-on velvet clothes; vintage ostrich plumes for hair; 1997, made by author. $250.

Right: Wooden peg doll: 11.5 inches; wooden doll like those featured in the Florence Upton books. Appears to be circa 1920. $175.

Plate: 17.5 inches; marked "Paul Pastaud Ursine Rue Jules Nariac." French Limoges; circa 1920. $95-125. (*Terri Kovacs collection*)

China mustard or jam pot: 4 inches; showing scenes based on Florence Upton's work; German; circa 1900. $450.

Golly cup and saucer; china; probably made in Germany; no marks; circa 1900. $165-185.

Platter: 7.5 x 10.5 inches; Alfred Meaken, England; Royal marigold pattern; early 1900s. $175-200. (*Terri Kovacs collection*)

Baby bowl: 5.5 inches; familiar scene found on a variety of children's dishes; made in Czechoslovakia; circa 1920. $75-100.

Baby dish: charming scene of a boy teaching Golliwoggs to be soldiers; Bisto china; England; circa 1920. $350.

Golliwogg bowl and plate: 6.5 and 8 inches; circa 1920; china featuring children with toys and animals as well as a Golliwogg; made in the United States by Schammell Lamberton. $65-75 each.

Golly bowl: made in Japan; circa 1920; unusual treatment. $168. (*Romy Roeder collection*)

Right: Golliwogg tea set; service for four; fifteen pieces total; marked Rudolstadt, Germany; circa 1920. $500.

Baby feeding bowl; circa 1920; made in England. $145. Egg cup; made in Japan. $26. (*Romy Roeder collection*)

China sandwich plate: 12.5 x 6 inches; initialed "J A"; British. A well-known British dealer, who has sold many pieces of china initialed "J A" and attributed to Joan Allen, includes a letterhead accounting of the artist with each purchase. This states that she attended St. Martin's Art School, eventually located in Stoke-on-Trent as a free-lance illustrator and counted, among others, clients such as Clarice Cliff and Shelley China (in the 1940s) He further informs us that Allen was a poet as well, and died in 1972. This information, however, cannot be considered a provenance unless further documentation is obtained. $375-400.

Below: China plate: 8.5 inches; initialed "J A" and attributed to Joan Allen; incorporates Gollies, Teddies, and Sunny Jim, a soap-product logo. The plate reads "Dig for Victory/Eat Well and Live Longer." This refers to wartime home vegetable gardens. $425.

China honey pot: 4 inches, initialed "J A" and attributed to Joan Allen; England. $125-150.

China baby feeder: 3 inches with spout and handle; initialed "J A" and attributed to Joan Allen. $225-250.

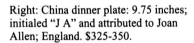

Right: China dinner plate: 9.75 inches; initialed "J A" and attributed to Joan Allen; England. $325-350.

China trivet: 6.25 x 7.5 inches; initialed "J A" and attributed to Joan Allen; England; $250-275.

China plate: 10 inches; initialed "J A" and attributed to Joan Allen; England; Golliwoggs, Sunny Jim, and dressed teddies. $550.

China egg cups: 2.25 inches; initialed "J A" and attributed to Joan Allen; England, 1940s. $75 each.

China mug: 4 inches; initialed "J A" and attributed to Joan Allen; England; 1940s. $195.

China mug: 4 inches; initialed "J A" and attributed to Joan Allen; England, 1940s. $175.

Left: China mug: 4 inches; initialed "J A" and attributed to Joan Allen; England, 1940s. Includes Rupert Bear. $195.

Left: China container: 3.5 inches; initialed "J A" and attributed to Joan Allen; England, 1940s. $125.

Right: China tumbler: 3.5 inches; initialed "J A" and attributed to Joan Allen; England, 1940s. $125.

Teddy and Golli plate: 9.75 inches; hand painted in England in the style of Joan Allen. $325.

Money box shaped like a mushroom; made by Colour-Box; 1994. $50. (*Terri Kovacs collection*)

Egg cup by Colour-Box; 1994; $50. Baby cup with verse on the back: 1994; made by Colour-Box; $40. Three-piece set marked "Colour-Box tale of Teddies Queen's Fine Bone China;" made in England; 1994. $100. (*Terri Kovacs collection*)

British pie funnel: 4 inches; glazed ceramic; original design by small potter in the English countryside; 1995. $40.

Golliwogg china tea set: made for the Toy Store in Toledo, Ohio, in 1996; showing the Steiff Golliwoggs made for the annual Steiff-sponsored festival in Toledo; 1996; limited edition of 1,000. $65.

Robertson's truck: made by Dinky Guy; circa 1955. $500-550. (*David Worland collection*)

Robertson plastic display: used in shops; shown with a jar of Golden Shred Marmalade. $200.

Golden Shred car: 3 inches; made by Days-Gone for Robertson's, purveyor of marmalade.

Robertson's store sign: large cardboard advertisement for Golden Shred Marmalade. $200-250. (*David Worland collection*)

Robertson's store sign: 5 x 7 inches; made of celluloid; free standing. $150-200. (*David Worland collection*)

Robertson's china platter and mug: premiums for the marmalade and jam company; circa 1996; made by MacDonald, England. $65-90.

Plastic Robertson's apron: adult size; advertising Golden Shred Marmalade. $150.

Robertson's china teapot and potpourri jar: premiums made about 1996 for the marmalade and jar company; made by MacDonald, England. $90-95 each.

Robertson egg cup: 3.75 inches; china; probably used as a memento at a sailing club; Printed on bottom "Made by the Silver Crane Co. By kind permission of Robertson's ;" circa 1970. $95.

Sterling rattle: 2 inches; British; 1909; one bell is missing. $350.

Marionette charm: Enameled gold; three dimensional; loop for hanging; with original glassine envelope; circa 1930. $125 up. Golly and marionette charm bracelet: 7.25 inches long; rare in this complete form; each design is under 3 centimeters; circa 1930. $400-450. Victorian gold charm: 1.25 centimeters; 9 karat gold. $300-350. (*Terri Kovacs collection*)

Le Golliwogg perfume bottle: glass with all labels; sealskin hair on stopper; attractive satin-lined box; missing lid; made by Vigny, Paris. 1920. $395.

Vigny perfume bottles: circa 1930 bottle with molded glass stopper; circa 1920 bottles with sealskin hair on the stoppers; the smallest is complete with a satin-lined box; called "Golliwogg;" made in France. $450-550.

Perfume Bottle: 4.25 inches; girl Golly wearing a yellow felt hat; frosted glass; appears to be about 1920. $250. (*Terri Kovacs collection*)

187

Greeting card: 5 inches; Golliwogg wearing a sandwich sign that reads, "Thumbs Up." Inside message reads, "Best Wishes for a Happy Christmas;" circa 1915. $75-95.

Golliwogg Pantin: 11 inches; Raphael Tuck pantin of a Golliwogg with a smaller version in each hand; beautifully colored; circa 1905. $550. (*David Worland collection*)

Left: Raphael Tuck rocker: 8.5 x 9.5 inches; British; circa1900; card is fashioned so that it rocks back and forth; verse message on back. $100-150. (*Terri Kovacs collection*)

Jolly Golly: 10 inches; dancing illusion figure; original envelope with instructions; circa 1920. $150-175. (*Terri Kovacs collection*)

Postcard: Fifi the Militant; political item; circa 1911. (*Susan Brown Nicholson collection*) No price available.

Golliwogg Card with panorama: 6 inches; colorful with black-and-white fold-out scenes of Christmas drawings; includes Father Christmas and cats by Louis Wain; Printed by Valentine & Sons Ltd.; Dundee and London; circa 1910. $100-125.

Golly panorama postcard with tab that pulls up and down and features accordian-shaped panorama of a resort in Margate; Printed in England, 1912. $90-100.

Agnes Richardson postcard with birthday greeting; British; 1917. $25. (*Maria Bluni collection*)

Panorama fold-out pictures.

189

New Year postcard: Unusual Golly with white hair is shown on a horse; circa 1900. $25-30. (*Maria Bluni collection*)

HUSH!

Chut !

Pattern book: contains information for making a Golliwogg-bear combination and other Golliwogg dolls; British; circa 1920. $75-95.

Mabel Lucie Attwell postcard: postmarked 1927; message written in French. $25-30. (*Maria Bluni collection*)

LITTLE GIRL: "AND I CAN'T TAKE MY BEST DOLLY TO HEAVEN?"
NURSE: "NO! DEAR."
LITTLE GIRL: "WELL I SUPPOSE I'LL HAVE TO TAKE MY GOLLY AND GO TO HELL."

Back cover of pattern book showing the Golly-Bear.

Postcard with message on front: Little Girl, "And I can't take my best Dolly to Heaven?" Nurse, "No! Dear." Little Girl: "Well, I suppose I'll have to take my Golly and go to Hell." Postmarked Dublin, 1919. $25. (*Maria Bluni collection*)

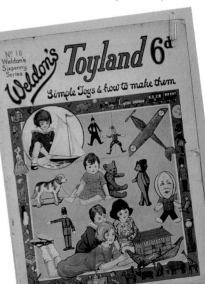

Framed Print "Toyland Holiday:" 22 x 24 inches; colorful Print of a Teddy driving a train with a Golliwogg and other toys as passengers and another Golly can be seen in the background; Label on back reads "For New Brighton Area Jointure Schools/New Brighton, Pa." Art by Brett; circa 1920. $175-200.

Right: Easter egg holder: 4.25 x 6 inches; hollowed-out space in back of the card can hold an egg; probably German; circa 1935. $65-75. (*Terri Kovacs collection*)

Golly bookmark: 6 inches; heavy paper with ribbon trim; circa 1935; complete with envelope. $79.

Left: Golli/Teddy collage: 9 x 12 inches; hand-painted watercolor background; cut-out child and toys are applied in an attractive manner; circa 1929. $85-100.

Right: Sheet music: "Dancing Golliwogg;" Beal Stuttard & Co. Ltd., London; by Alan Saville; ©1934. $45-50. (*Terri Kovacs collection*)

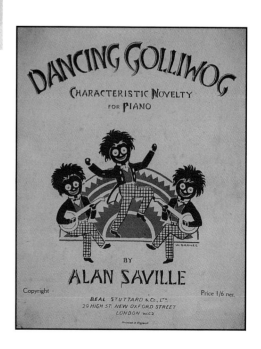

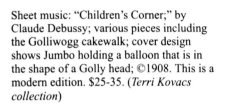

Sheet music: "Golliwogg Parade;" The Willis Music Co., Cinncinnatti, Ohio; circa 1950. $25-35. (*Terri Kovacs collection*)

Sheet music: "Children's Corner;" by Claude Debussy; various pieces including the Golliwogg cakewalk; cover design shows Jumbo holding a balloon that is in the shape of a Golly head; ©1908. This is a modern edition. $25-35. (*Terri Kovacs collection*)

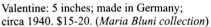

Right: Golly scorecard and pencil for playing Whist (bridge); circa 1940. $90-100.

Notepaper: pastel paper with matching envelopes; includes ten toy stamps; circa 1940. $75. (*Terri Kovacs collection*)

Valentine: 5 inches; made in Germany; circa 1940. $15-20. (*Maria Bluni collection*)

Australian *Cosies-Toys and Novelties* magazine: no date but appears to be from the 50s. $18-26. (*Dot Gillett collection*)

The New Idea magazine: November 10, 1954 issue showing knitted Golliwogg; instructions inside; $30-35. (*Dot Gillett collection*)

Instructions for "Hubshee," found in the *Cosies* magazine. (*Dot Gillett collection*)

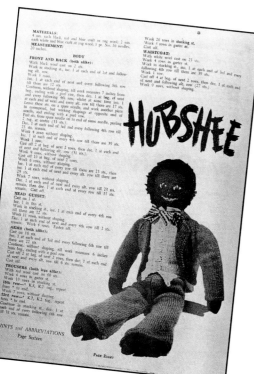

Knitted Golliwogg: made from instructions in *The New Idea Magazine.* $48-56. (*Dot Gillett collection*)

Knitted "Hubshee:" made from instructions in the *Cosies* magazine. $34-41. (*Dot Gillett collection*)

Match cover from the Golliwogg Lounge at the Sheraton Hotel in New York City

Left: Santa lithograph: 12 inches; paper on cardboard with standard on back; a Golliwogg is shown in the back pack; probably British; circa 1950. $95-100. (*Maria Bluni collection*)

Greeting card given to conventioneers at the 10th Festival of Steiff in 1995: The Golliwogg was the event theme; especially Printed and signed by Jorg Juninger of the Steiff Co. in Germany.

Golliwogg hankerchiefs: 13.5 inches square: two of three in a series; Golliwoggs are featured in the manner of "Ten Little Indians;" hankie with number six and seven is missing; rare and desirable; Reg. # 41780. and Reg. # 41779; circa 1900. $375-425 pair.

Knit pattern book: Sirdar Sunshine Series; patterns for child's cardigan, trousers, and short-sleeve sweater; circa 1960. $50-75.

Nursery rug: 22 x 44 inches; British Axminster weave; features a clown, ball, drums, and a train as well as a Golliwogg; circa 1925. $400-plus.

Uncut Golliwogg bib: 14 x 20 inches; Printed on cotton; shows colorful figures from Upton books; manufactured by Windsor Print Works, North Adams, Massachussets; pictures reproduced from the Golliwogg Books published by Longman's Green & Co, New York; circa 1900. $300-plus.

Rug: 23 x 36 inches; titled "All Aboard;" labeled carpets by Worth; circa 1930. $350-400. (*Terri Kovacs collection*)

Golliwogg socks shown with ad that appeared in *Woman's Day* magazine dated October 8, 1956. Socks were made by Branross Pty. Ltd., Melbourne, Australia. $150. (*Dot Gillett collection*)

Golliwogg Vienna bronzes: 1 inch; Golli drags Peg by one arm. She is missing a leg and he holds that under one arm. The other one is a figure of a Dutch doll sitting. Circa 1910. $150 each.

Golly apron in canvas-type fabric with black-and-white Print; artist rendition; made in Australia; 1990s. $25-35.

Vienna bronze: 1.5 inches; two Golliwoggs and a Peg doll; sealskin hair; circa 1900. $300-plus.

Vienna bronze: 1.5 inches; three Golliwoggs with joined hands; sealskin hair; circa 1900. $300-plus.

Tin stickpin: .75 inches. painted; circa 1915. $50. (*Becky Mucchetti collection*)

Golliwogg Christmas cake tin: 4 inches; octagonal shape with colorful graphics; "Jacob's Biscuits" impressed on bottom; Circa 1940. $225.

Australian cookie tin: 8 x 5 inches; made by A. W. Allen Ltd., Melbourne. "Sweet Dreams" Printed on the front; 1950s. $56. (*Dot Gillett collection*)

Golliwogg chocolate cookies; made in Australia by Arnott's.

Cookie tin: 6 inches on each side; no marks; 1950s; also came in yellow but green is harder to locate. $112-plus. (*Dot Gillett collection*)

Australian toffee tin: 5 inches; imprinted on back "Embassy expressly packed for G. J. Coles & Coy Ltd, Melbourne." $48. (*Dot Gillett collection*)

Pin cushion: 1 inch; molded metal; Golly has nappy hair and side-glancing eyes; dating uncertain. $55-65. (*Terri Kovacs collection*)

Child's sewing box: 5.5 x 4.5 x 2 inches; wood with paper lithograph; design by Agnes Richardson; removeable tray for sewing items; circa 1920. $75-100. (*Terri Kovacs collection*)

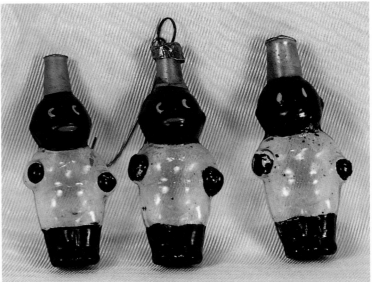

Christmas ornaments: 2.25 inches; clear glass bodies take on the color of any colored bulb behind it; Germany; circa 1910. $55-75 each. (*Terri Kovacs collection*)

Right: Firecrackers: registered by the Yan Kee Firecracker Mfg. Co., Hong Kong and Canton; ten firecrackers; pre-1950. $200-250.

Squeak Toy: 6.75 inches; molded rubber; British; circa 1950. $75-95. (*Terri Kovacs collection*)

Topplem Golliwoggs game: a game of skill in which wooden balls are placed on a springboard and aimed at the Gollys; made by Royal Series; circa 1910. $495.

Board game opened.

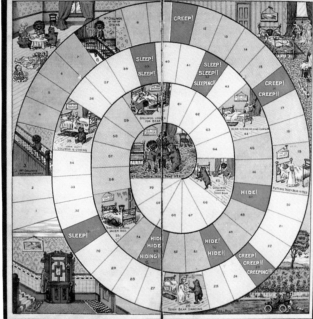

Golliwogg Jumping Jack: 6 inches; wood with paper overlay; British; circa 1905. $275-plus. (*David Worland collection*)

Golliwogg and the Teddy Bears board game: Ariel Reg'd; showing the alliance between the Golly and the Teddy; only the colorful board remains; circa 1908. $375-400.

Metal drum: 6.25 inches; made in England; paper overlay; circa 1910. $295.

Nesting blocks: up to 3.5 inches; colored paper over cardboard; four blocks in the set; only the largest and outer block shows a Golliwogg; circa 1930. $125.

Golliwogg bank: 6 inches; lightweight metal painted in vivid colors (probably repainted); British; circa 1910. $225.

Wooden blocks puzzle: 8 x 10 inches; light wood covered with lithographed paper; child holds a Golly girl and Peg dolls may be seen in the wagon; circa 1910. $300-350. (*Terri Kovacs collection*)

Left: Golly Jack-in-the-Box: 4 inches square; wood box that is wood burned and colored; wooden head; yarn hair; cotton clothes; circa 1915. $265.

Right: Paper over cardboard blocks forms a puzzle; Charlie Chaplin is shown in a Jack-in-the-box and a Golliwogg hangs from the Christmas tree; circa 1930. $125.

British spinning top: appears to be one of the Noddy products; shows a Golli, a teddy, two elves, and a few toys; circa 1950. $90-120.

Musical toy: 5 inches; metal toy with Golli graphics; music is activated by turning wooden knob at the top; made in Germany; circa 1950. $150-175.

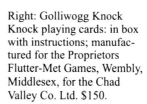

Right: Golliwogg Knock Knock playing cards: in box with instructions; manufactured for the Proprietors Flutter-Met Games, Wembly, Middlesex, for the Chad Valley Co. Ltd. $150.

Robertson bridge set: vinyl case; contains two sets of cards, scorepad, and pencil; complete in box; circa 1980. $125

The Toy Shop Game: British; 1950s. $75-100. (*David Worland collection*)

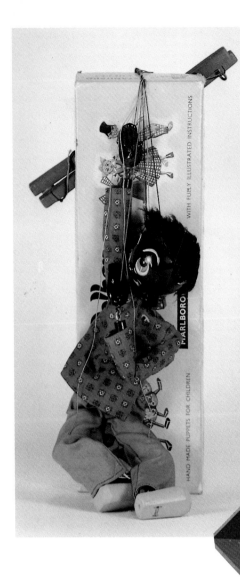

Left: Marionette: 12 inches; produced by the well-known British puppet maker Pelham; this Golliwogg is mint-in-the-box; circa 1960. $250-plus.

Right: Golliwogg Jack-in-the-box: 10 inches; felt and velvet Golli in wooden box; made by Dean's of England; 1990s. $75.

Right: Ring Toss Game: Paper graphic on plywood with rubber quoits; made in Finland for Begnat; circa 1960. $250+.

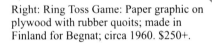

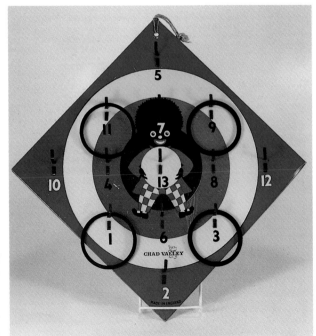

Left: Ring toss game: made by Chad Valley, England; circa 1950. $95-150. (*Terri Kovacs collection*)

Right: Figurine: 6 inches; china Golly sitting on a pillow; by designer Clarice Cliff who worked in several British china factories after 1920; this extremely rare piece is marked "Bizarre by Clarice Cliff;" potter is Kinson Ltd. $2,200.

Golly G and Teddy B figurine: 3 inches; a Colour Box miniature made for the Toy Store in Toledo, Ohio; designed by Peter Fagan; 1995; limited edition. $65.

Author and "Big" Golliwoggs: taken at the Steiff Festival in Toledo in 1995 when the theme was Golliwoggs. Dressed to the "Golly nines" are Steiff representative Dick Frantz and Karl Gibbons owner of Theodore's Emporium in London.

Dot Gillett, probably Australia's most avid Golly collector, is shown wearing a circa-1950, hand-painted trenchcoat.

Dot Gillett's suit jacket is not only decorated with characters from the Noddy books, but is battery wired so that the eyes light up.

The Golly collection of long-time enthusiast Bill Boyd. (*Photo courtesy of Bill Boyd*)

Chapter VII
The Bear Facts

The Three Bears

Book: *The Three Bears*: ©1888 by McLoughlin, New York; Little Folk Series; colorful graphics. $195.

Once upon a time, at the edge of a forest, there lived three bears. The cottage where they dwelt was charming, rose trellised, and neat as a pin due to the ministration of Mama Bear. So goes the tale enjoyed by generations of children the world over. The story evolved over the years according to the whims of writers, artists, and publishers. The Three Bears appear to have made their debut in verse form as early as 1831 with the culprit featured as a witch rather than a child. When the books took on a moralistic message the naughty girl was variously known as Silverhair, Silverlocks, Goldenhair, Goldenlocks, and finally the familiar Goldilocks. The bruins also changed titles as well, sometimes referred to as Great, Medium and Little Bear. At first they walked on all four feet and thus appeared in realistic form. Now, of course, we always think of them as upright, dressed, and called Papa, Mama, and Baby Bear.

Countless books have been Printed regularly and in several languages and formats. The publishing presentations have included hard cover, paper, the almost indestructible linen cloth, and pop-ups. Since a goodly number of fine artists have leant their talents to this enterprise, many of the books have stunning graphics. Promotional booklets are yet another bit of ephemera with advertisers as diverse as automobile axles and oatmeal, enticing buyers with a three-bear motif.

Ironically, bears as playthings have not been *plentifully* manufactured. A few companies such as Dean's in England and Knickerbocker in the United States developed sets in the 1930s. The 1932 F A O Schwarz catalogue featured a book along with a plush, dressed three-bear family. They ranged in size from 8.25 inches to 14 inches and could be purchased for less than sixteen dollars a set. I expect that seemed expensive during the depression era. Kellogg's, Cranston Print Works, and V. I. P. Fabrics have offered cut, sew, and stuffed models at various times. Robert Raikes, working with Applause, designed a set in the 1980s mounted on a wooden base. In 1984, the Steiff Company introduced a limited edition with a Goldilocks created by doll artist Suzanne Gibson, and the following year offered a smaller variation.

The three bears theme, however, is found on incalculable memorabilia treasures. Toys, puzzles, games, and china are but a few of the many articles that can be amassed to form an eclectic display.

Books: *The Three Bears* by W. B. Conkey; circa 1900; child referred to as Silverlocks. $75. And *The Three Bears*; Whitman Publishing; circa 1925; child referred to as Goldilocks. $75.

Book: *The Story of the Three Bears:* Linenette; Little Kitten Series; published by McLoughlin Bros., New York; pre-1900. $125.

Book: *All About the Three Bears*: small hardcover edition; illustrated by L. Kirby-Parrish and Dick Hartley; published by Cupples & Leon Co., New York; ©1914; one in a series. $60-65.

Book: *The Three Bears:* Softcover; Father Tuck's Nursery Tales Series; published by Raphael Tuck & Sons Ltd., London; circa 1890. $50-60.

The Three Bears: artwork by Frances Brundage; published by Saalfield, Akron, Ohio; no date; circa 1915. $50-55.

Figural book: small format; published by Valentine & Sons Ltd. circa 1920. $45-50.

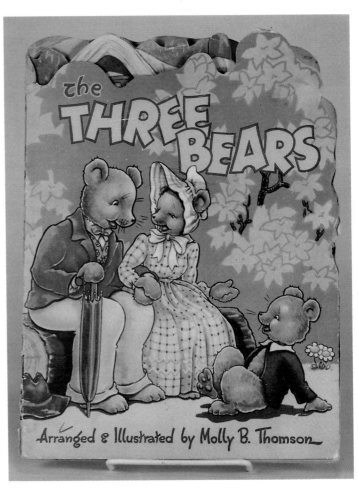

Book: *The Three Bears*: paper; figural format; Collins Clear Type Press; British; circa 1930; Baby Bear has a Golly toy. $45-50. (*Terri Kovacs collection*)

" Somebody's been sleeping in MY bed," growled Mummy Bear. Baby Bear shouted, "Somebody's been sleeping in MY bed and

"She's STILL THERE!!!!!"

Page from Three Bears figural book showing a Golliwogg.

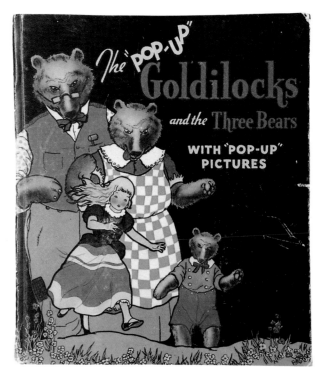

The "Pop-Up" Goldilocks and the Three Bears: published by Blue Ribbon Press; 1934; American. $75-80.

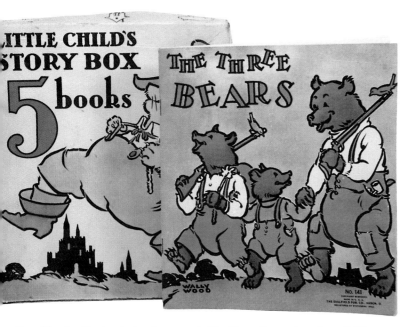

Boxed books: five books in a box; one is *The Three Bears;* American; 1937; published by Saalfield. $20-25.

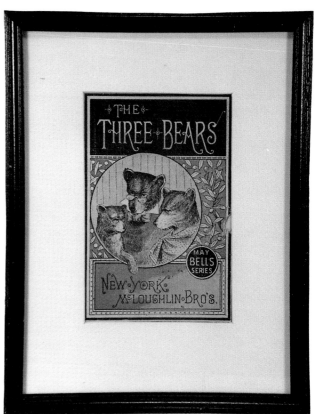

The Three Bears: Small paper book matted and framed; published by McLoughlin Bros; May Bells Series; circa 1890. $70-75.

The Three Bears: Merril Publishing Co., Chicago; 1942. $18-20.

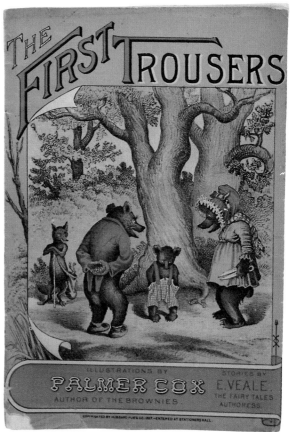

The First Trousers: paper format; advertising giveaway by the Boston Store. Illustrated by Palmer Cox; Hubbard Publishing Co., 1897. A variation on the three bears theme. $90.

Advertising booklet: *Little Golden Hair*: colorful tale of the Three Bears; advertising Krell Pianos, though the same booklet has been used for other products; 1901. $80-90.

Reverse side of booklet showing Krell advertisement.

Advertising booklet: *Bright Eyes and the Three Bears*; circa 1890; advertises H-O Oatmeal. $60-70.

Page from booklet showing the oatmeal ad.

Advertising booklet: *Little Golden Hair*; Mrs. Winslow's Soothing Syrup for teething children; 1901; the same booklet was used by several different companies. $90.

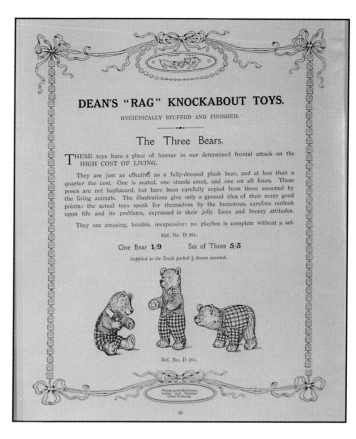

Catalog page describing the three bears; Dean's "Rag" Knockabout Toys, England. 1920.

Kellogg's Goldilocks from *The Three Bears*: Goldilocks, Papa, Mama, and Johnny bear are Printed on cloth; designed to be cut, sewn, and stuffed by the home sewer. ©1926. $500 set.

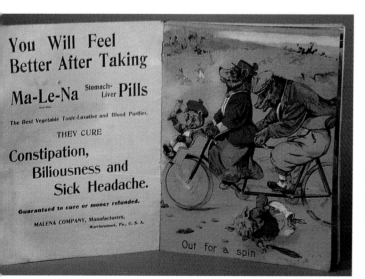

Advertising booklet: A variation on the Three Bears theme entitled *The Animal Outing*; for Ma-Le-Na Stomach Liver Pills; colorful; as shown in illustrated page; circa 1910. $50-60.

Kellogg's Papa Bear.

Kellogg's Johnny Bear (Baby Bear)

Kellogg's Mama Bear.

These two bears give the impression of each being part of a three bears trio. Both look like Papa bear. One is embroidered on linen, the other has a mohair head and fabric made-on clothing; circa 1925-1930. $60-125.

Goldilocks and the Three Bears: 9-14 inches. The Bears are circa 1930 Steiffs that have been altered, adapted, and strung, probably by a puppeteer, so as to perform as marionettes. They are dressed and operate beautifully via wooden cross bars. Goldilocks has a pressed felt face and a composition body; she is possibly an original marionette. Offered December 1996 by Christie's auction house, London. (*Photo courtesy of Christie's, London*)

The Three Bears: 9 in, 10 in, 11 inches Mama, Papa and Baby Bear (called Boobsie;) plush with googly roll-around eyes; cotton and felt clothes; two largest have tags; mint in box; circa 1935. Knickerbocker Toy Co. $600.

Handmade bears: 8, 10, and 12 inches; cotton and felt with embroidered features, soft stuffed; appearance suggests a commercial pattern; circa 1935;. $35-45.

Steiff Goldilocks and the Three Bears: doll by Suzanne Gibson; bears range in sizes from 9.25-13 inches; limited edition of 2,000 pieces; 1984. $700.

The Three Bears mug: 4 inches; Shelley china, England; circa 1900. $125.

The Three Bears: designed by Robert Raikes, made by Applause; plush with carved faces on wooden base; all tags intact; 1980s. $750-plus.

The Three Bears by artist Bonnie Butler Jonus; imaginatively accessorized; 1996. No price available. (*Photo courtesy of Bonnie Butler Jonus*)

The Three Bears plate: 8.25 inches; charming scene with poem at top, "Silverhair—I declare you have broken bruins chair! When they reach their home (or lair) When they see the havoc there: Twill be more than they can bear." Made by Shelley; British; circa 1900. $175-200.

The Three Bears plate: 6.5 inches; impressed amber; 1920s. $75.

Doll suitcase: 7 inches; circa 1930. $75-85. (*Lorraine Oakley collection*)

The Three Bears plate: 5 inches; circa 1935. $45-50.

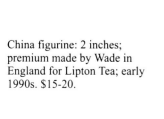

China figurine: 2 inches; premium made by Wade in England for Lipton Tea; early 1990s. $15-20.

Childs wooden chair painted yellow (worn) with color transfer of Papa and Baby Bear; American; circa 1935. $95-100.

The Three Bears blocks: paper lithographed on wood blocks; makes six scenes, some with bears; scene assembled shows Golliwogg in foreground; complete with cloth book; in box; artist Altiora Peta; circa 1895; Printed in Bavaria. $475-500.

Wooden block: 2 inches square; one of a set; showing bears in silhouette; circa 1935. $10-12.

The Three Bears series: Three sets of chromolithographs on wooden, double-sized puzzles telling the story along with original book; a McLoughlin Young Folk series; ©1888; the original box still retains the Hamley's Toy store warehouse sticker; offered at auction in December 1996 by Christie's, London. (*Photo courtesy of Christie's, London*)

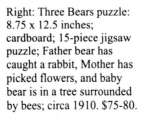

Left: The Three Bears game: wooden game board; Telegame series; McLoughlin; circa 1890. $200-250.

Right: Three Bears puzzle: 8.75 x 12.5 inches; cardboard; 15-piece jigsaw puzzle; Father bear has caught a rabbit, Mother has picked flowers, and baby bear is in a tree surrounded by bees; circa 1910. $75-80.

Right: The Three Bears puzzle: 13 x 18 inches; circa 1920. $125.
Center right: The Three Bears puzzle: 13 x 18 inches; circa 1920. $125.
Bottom right: Photo of The Three Bears puzzle: 13 x 18 inches; circa 1920. $125.

The Three Bears puzzle: 11 x 8.5 inches; 12-piece puzzle; paper lithographed on cardboard; circa 1915; marked "S. G. S. & Co." $20-25.

TWO PUZZLES IN THIS BOX

MADMAR
Picture Puzzle
STORY BOOK SERIES
MANUFACTURED BY
Madmar Quality Co.,
Utica, N.Y.
No. 300

Getting ready for the walk.

Puzzles: 6.5 x 8.5 inches; two puzzles in box; American; Madmar Quality Co.; circa 1920. $85-90.

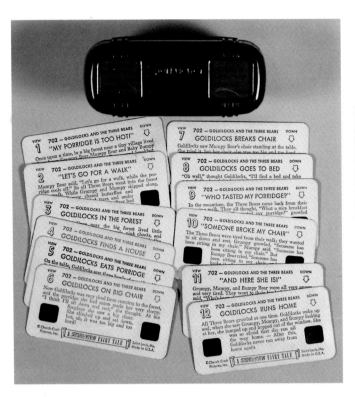

A delightful 3D viewer of Goldilocks and The Three Bears; viewer and 12 cards; American; circa 1930; St. Louis, Missouri; Church Craft Pictures Inc. $160-170.

Souvenir tip tray: 4 inches; The Three Bears; white metal; bears in raised relief; 1,000 Animals/Lake Placid, New York; circa 1920; marked "Japan 1/19/8." $40-45.

The Three Bears bank: 5 inches; coppery metal; circa 1930; American; slot on the back for coins. $86-95.

Magazine page: to be cut and assembled for play; by Helen Pettes; circa 1920. $40-45.

Cutouts: Showing Goldilocks in bed, the three bears, baby bear's chair and the porridge-laden table; some parts probably missing; 1940s. $10.

Poster: 20 x 30 inches; Vaudeville poster; ca.1920. $250. (*Marsha Bohling collection*)

The Three Bears writing tablet: paper tablet with the story on the inside cover. The child is referred to as Goldenlocks; circa 1935. $45.

The Three Bears hanky: designed by Mabel Lucie Atwell; circa 1920. $90.

The Three Bears quilt: 35 x 50 inches Colorful quilt, pre-colored and outline embroidered; American; circa 1940. $100-125.

The Three Bears drapery: cotton fabric Printed with scenes suitable for a child's room; circa 1950. $20-25.

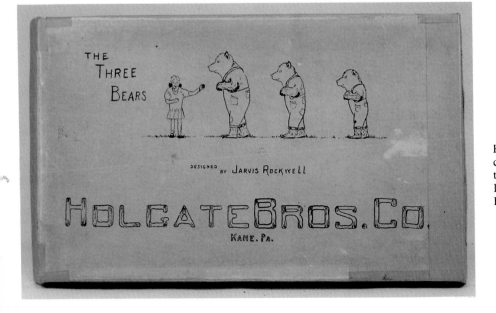

Holgate boxed set showing the lid of the box that contains a complete set of wooden Three Bears toys. This is the company's first "Educational Line" on the market and was designed by Jarvis Rockwell; circa 1930. $900-1,000.

Log cabin and three beds from the Holgate set.

Table, three chairs, and three bowls of porridge from the Holgate set.

Papa, Mama, baby, and Goldilocks from the Holgate set.

Punkinhead

Book: *Punkinhead in Santa's Workshop*: paper; given to children; ©1950. $20-25. (*Donna McPherson collection*)

An interesting concept was conceived in 1947 by the advertising departments of Eaton's stores in Toronto, Ontario, and Winnipeg, Manitoba Canada. Retailers consistently strive to attract new customers and retain their regulars with varied products and fresh marketing ideas. At this particular meeting, work was begun to generate interest and excitement for the store's annual Christmas parade. Animals have always been beloved by every age group and bears were deemed a sure-fire winner. With this in mind, a teddy was decided upon and, additionally, it was decided that he should be slightly pathetic. Anything that stirs the emotions and pulls at one's heart strings cannot help but be popular.

So "Punkinhead—The Sad Little Bear" became a reality. He made his first appearance in the 1947 parade and was an instant sensation. The parade figure was two feet tall, wore short trousers, and weighed in at four pounds. What made him sad? Well, unlike other bears, this fanciful creature had an unruly thatch of hair growing out of the top of his head. Surely that was enough to make any teddy bear weep. (Talk about bad hair days!) Even Santa was moved by the bear's despair and made him his special helper. Punkinhead turned into a hero and ultimately saved the parade.

What started as an advertising gimmick became a merchandising bonanza. His launch was so successful that he became Eaton's trademark and was showcased in nearly every department. Punkinhead was copyrighted in 1948 and items of every description filled the shelves, including a teddy bear made by Merrythought of England.

The first of the fourteen books that were ultimately published was called *The Sad Little Bear*. The story was written by the advertising department personnel in Toronto and the Winnipeg office commissioned Disney artist Charles Thorson to do the illustrations. Usually the volume comes first, but in this instance the positions were reversed. About the same time a record album was released, relating further tales of Punkinhead's adventurous exploits.

Punkinhead remained Eaton's most successful product for many years. In 1967, twenty years after his debut, their catalog listed twenty-nine items. They included three bears in sizes 10, 16, and 23 inches, a twenty-piece tea set, a paint box, rubber balls in two sizes, a baby rocker, a three-piece breakfast set, a bank, and a rubber doll as well as a stamped cotton model. Clothing for children consisted of slipper socks, fur-trimmed slippers, pajamas, sweatshirts, plastic bibs, aprons, sweaters, handbags, and a handkerchief book with five hankies and pictures to match. It was possible to accessorize a child's room, as well, with a lamp, pictures, and a rug. Additionally, one could dazzle one's friend with a watch and even tie packages with red or green ribbon emblazoned with his portrait and a cheery message. All of the products had Punkinhead featured in various poses, and last but not least, a new story book was included with each order. Prices ranged from 35 cents for a face cloth to $10.95 for the largest stuffed bear.

The target audience was designed to attract not only children, but adults as well, and in this they were also successful. A revival occurred on Punkinhead's fortieth anniversary, inspiring renewed interest in the adult marketplace. Collectors who owned this endearing bear as a childhood toy hung on to it, no matter how tattered, and soon became avid in the pursuit of other Punkinhead memorabilia.

Book: *How Punkinhead Came to Toyland*: Paper format; given to children with Eaton's compliments; ©1953. $25-30. (*Donna McPherson collection*)

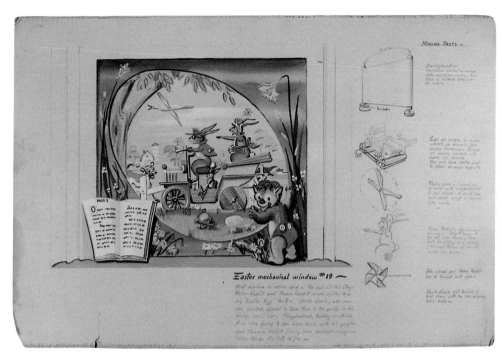

Department store window #1: Color rendition and diagrams describing how the mechanism is to be built and operated. Punkinhead to be 4-feet tall and the other animals to range in sizes from 18 inches to 3 feet. Punkinhead and Peter Rabbit are featured. For Easter 1947. $700 set of four. (*Donna McPherson collection*)

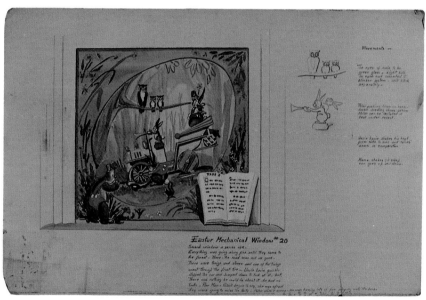

Department store window #2 showing Punkinhead, rabbits, and owls with eyes that light up.

Department store window # 3.

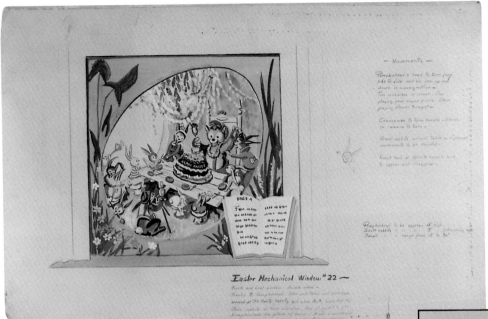

Left: Department store window # 4; the fourth and last window in the panoply.

Easter Mechanical Window #22

Below: Phonograph record: circa 1950; relates the complete Punkinhead story. $25-30. (*Donna McPherson collection*)

Book: *Punkinhead and His Toy Workshop Adventure*: paper; given to children; ©1954. $15-20. (*Donna McPherson collection*)

THE STORY OF
Punkinhead

Once upon a time there was a little bear who had a big woolly tuft in the middle of his head. Everybody laughed at him and called him "Punkinhead" and this made him very sad.

One day Santa Claus came to the forest, where the bears lived, on his way to Toyland. What excitement! Everyone had honey sodas to celebrate. One important clown drank so many he got a tummy ache and had to go to bed.

"Oh dear," said Santa Claus, "he is so important but we can't wait for him to get better or we'll be late."

"Maybe one of the little bears could take his place," said the Fairy Queen.

So one little bear tried on the suit. It fit just right. But that hat—his head was so smooth—it fell right off! A second little bear tried and it fell off him too.

"If only the Fairy Queen could wave her magic wand and make a lock of hair stand up in the middle," said Jack Frost.

"A lock of hair," said the bears, "in the middle!" and they scampered off to find "Punkinhead." When they found him, they pushed and pulled and hurried him back through Bear-Land Forest!

The clown suit fit just right. And the hat—it fit too! Because Punkinhead's lock of hair held it there. "Ho, the very thing!" said Santa Claus and the Fairy Queen and Jack Frost.

Of course he was a shining star in Santa's Big Parade and Punkinhead, the sad little bear, became a very happy bear after all!

Copyright

Story that appears on the Punkinhead record jacket.

222

Punkinhead: 23 inches; paper mâché display piece; used at Eaton's Department Store in Canada; moveable arms, removeable felt pants; unusual; 1950s. $1,200-plus.

Right: British Merrythought *Punkinhead* bear: 20 inches; brown and gold mohair; white mohair tuft; velvet muzzle and feet; clear glass eyes; felt pads; excelsior and kapok filled; red felt shorts; all jointed; made exclusively for Eaton's Department Store in Toronto, Canada.; circa 1960. $1,500-plus.

Punkinhead: 16 inches; replaced pants; circa 1950; Merrythought label on foot; sold at auction in 1994 for approximately $1,575. (*Photo courtesy of Christie's, London*)

Left: British Merrythought *Punkinhead*: 12 inches; brown and gold mohair; velvet muzzle and feet; white mohair tuft; excelsior and kapok filled; clear glass eyes painted white on the back; all jointed; missing shorts; circa 1960. $600-plus. (*Susan Stanton Reid collection*)

Punkinhead: 10 inches; mohair; missing pants; made by Merrythought; circa 1960. $500. (*Donna McPherson collection*)

Below: Carnival-style Punkinhead: 21 inches sitting; not jointed, plush; plastic eyes, yarn nose, felt mouth partially missing; 1950s. $50-75. (*Donna McPherson collection*)

Punkinhead: 14 inches, not jointed, plush; plastic googly eyes; music box that winds from the back; 1960s. $35-45. (*Donna McPherson collection*)

Punkinhead: 15 inches; not jointed plush; plastic eyes and nose; vinyl hang tag Print ed in both British and French; made in Taiwan; 1970s. $50-60. (*Donna McPherson collection*)

Right: Punkinhead: 22 inches; mohair; plastic eyes; all jointed; felt mouth and nose; made by 24K, Quebec; 1970s. $350-plus. (*Donna McPherson collection*)

Some of the Punkinhead items available in the 1967 Eaton catalog.

Ancestor of Cheeky: 10 inches; replica, with minor changes, of Merrythought's early version of Punkinhead; called "Ancestor" because even though they produced the original, they could not use the name because Eaton's holds the copyright; 1987. $400-plus.

Punkinhead: 14 inches; not jointed, plush; wearing sweater with his name on it; tag is a small storybook entitled *The Surprise*; made in China; 1994. $40-50. (*Donna McPherson collection*)

Punkinhead tea set shown in the 1967 Eaton catalog.

Child-size platter and tureen: China; part of a set that includes service for four; transfer pattern; made in Japan; circa 1955. $425 set. (*Donna McPherson collection*)

Teapot, sugar, and creamer: part of a set that serves four. (*Donna McPherson collection*)

Cereal bowl: 5 inches in diameter; Punkinhead is three-dimentional and seems to hold the bowl; Sutton Ceramics, Canada; 1950s. $65-75. (*Donna McPherson collection*)

Plate, cup, and saucer: part of the service for four. (*Donna McPherson collection*)

Electric bottle warmer: for a baby; with Punkinhead design; mint-in-box; 1950s. $55-65. (*Donna McPherson collection*)

China bowl: 7 inches in diameter; blue with transfer design; Rideau Pottery, Canada; circa 1950. $40-50. (*Donna McPherson collection*)

Folding metal table: 24 x 24 inches; card-table style; for a child; colorful graphics; circa 1948. $75-100. (*Donna McPherson collection*)

Child's set of watercolors including brushes and many colors; 1960s. $45-50. (*Donna McPherson collection*)

Punkinhead and friends Print by Canadian artist Janice Keirstead; "Punky and Pals." Prints were made in 1992 and used as a giveaway poster by Eaton's Dept. Store. (*Donna McPherson collection*)

Punkinhead "Doctor and Patient" Print: watercolor painting by Canadian artist Janice Keirstead; limited edition of second Print in the series sold by Eaton's. (*Donna McPherson collection*)

Print of Punkinhead painting by Canadian artist Janice Keirstead; limited edition of 350; first picture. Four limited-edition Prints were contracted for by Eaton's to be issued for four consecutive years, but after two seasons the contract was cancelled. This Print was one of those sold. (*Donna McPherson collection*)

"Punkinhead the Artist" Print: limited edition of third painting by Canadian artist Janice Keirstead; Printed but not sold. (*Donna McPherson collection*)

Punkinhead's picnic Print: limited edition; fourth painting by Canadian artist Janice Keirstead, was not Printed except for twenty artist proofs. (*Donna McPherson collection*)

Paddington Bear

In 1956, Michael Bond presented his wife with a teddy bear he had purchased at Selfridge's Department Store. The bear was a successful gift for *he* soon was the recipient of gifts himself. The clothes he was outfitted with are now a signature as identifiable as his name. Paddington's duffle coat, slouch hat ,and suitcase suggested a traveler and it wasn't long before Bond's whimsical imagination took flight. It is not unusual for teddy collectors to indulge in a bit of fantasy and give a life to a favorite bruin. Michael's dream, however, was to put down a story on paper, not dreaming at the time that this and varied products would evolve into an industry.

A Bear Called Paddington was published in 1958. It told the tale of an accident-prone bear who arrived in London, via Paddington Station, all the way from darkest Peru. Attached to a toggle button on his coat was a tag with delivery instructions and a message to "please look after this bear." Paddington's love for marmalade and his attempts, as a foreigner, to learn the British way of life endeared him to readers everywhere. The book was so successful that a new adventure was published every year for the following decade. Additionally, six new collections came out between 1968 and 1981. Paperback items followed the hard copies along with birthday, pop-ups and various other novelties. Beginning in 1960, the books were published in the United States as well and translated into many foreign languages. As a tribute to the store where he was purchased, the twenty-fifth anniversary book was written especially for Selfridge's.

Paddington was not only featured on radio and television programs, but was the basis for a musical performed in England and Australia. The animated puppet series, first shown on the BBC in Britain, was eventually sold internationally.

Shirley Clarkson, founder of Gabrielle Designs, was granted a license to manufacture the first stuffed toy replica in 1972. It was she who outfitted Paddington with Wellington boots and Bond integrated them in subsequent books. At first only a 20-inch bear was released, but orders for him came so swiftly that the company started to produce other sizes and finally ceased making any *other* toys until 1985. Gabrielle also created Paddington's Aunt Lucy, the Peruvian relative who had cared for him before his journey to London. Three years after Gabrielle started making him, Eden Toys of New York obtained the rights to manufacture Paddington for the rest of the world. In the absence of tags, the two firms' products can be differentiated by the safety pin in the hat of British versions. Safety regulations in America precluded this feature.

Because fans clamored for more related objects, Michael Bond formed Paddington and Co. This business monitored the licensing of an enormous array of items, from board games to slippers and even chocolates. In fact, there were so many products that a store called "Paddington and Friends" opened in London in 1978, with branches in other cities.

The Gabrielle Company was reorganized in 1994 under new management. The total share holding was acquired by a new team and the firm will continue to charm us with new and exciting Paddington designs.

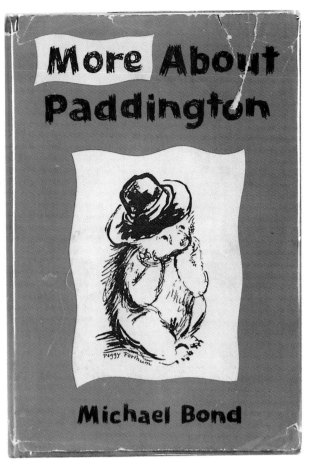

More About Paddington: hard cover with dust jacket; the second book; Michael Bond; illustrated by Peggy Fortnum; ©1959 Collins Publishing. $125.

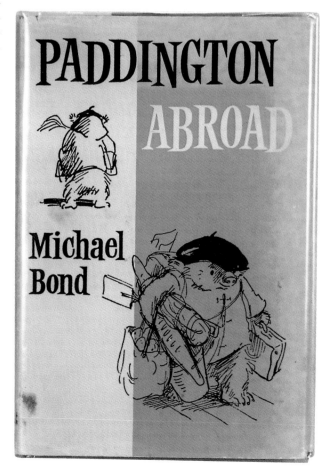

Book: *Paddington Abroad.* Hard cover with dust jacket; ©1961 Collins Publishing Co; by Michael Bond; illustrated by Peggy Fortnum. $95.

The Great Big Paddington Book: Large format; hardcover; by Michael Bond, Collins Publishing; ©1977. $65.

Right: Paddington Station sign.

Book: *Paddington's Shopping Trip* by Michael Bond; published by Starstream Products; 1980; paper format. $5-7.

Paddington gift kiosk at Paddington Station.

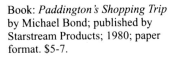

Paddington Station.

Paddington appeal bank: Paddington is found on many streets throughout England to collect money for childhood disease research.

Paddington: 19 inches; wearing traditional toggle coat, hat, and wellingtons; made by Eden Toys; 1970s. $250-275.

Paddington: 13 inches; traditional costume; made by Eden Toys; 1970s. $95-plus.

Paddington: 20 inches; Gabrielle archive product; made in 1972.

Left: Paddington: 18 inches; plush; wearing traditional clothing; the green coat was discontinued in 1977; made by Gabrielle Designs, England. $225-250.

Paddington: 20 inches; Gabrielle Archives; made in 1972.

Paddington: 20 inches; Gabrielle Designs; 1970s; all original. $245.

Paddington: 20 inches; Gabrielle Designs; 1970s; all original. $245.

Aunt Lucy: 20 inches; made by Gabrielle; all original; has coins in her "knickers;" 1970s. $225.

Aunt Lucy: 20 inches; made by Gabrielle; missing hat; has coins in her "knickers;" 1970s. $175.

Gabrielle Aunt Lucy: 20 inches; made in 1978; an example in this company's archives.

Gabrielle Paddingtons: 14 inches; ski-suited bears made in the mid 1980s; Gabrielle Archives.

Paddington: 18 inches; gold mohair; plastic eyes and nose; not jointed; dressed in felt with rubber boots; made by Gabrielle Designs Ltd., 1980. $175-200.

Rugby Paddington: 14 inches; Gabrielle Archives; 1981.

Golfing Paddington: 14 inches; Gabrielle Archives; 1980s.

Paddington in tuxedo: 14 inches; Gabrielle Archives; 1980s.

Paddington beanbag: 8 inches; plush; bean stuffed; felt clothes; 1980s; made by Gabrielle. $50-60.

Paddington: 14 inches; Gabrielle Designs; circa 1980. $125.

Paddington: 14 inches; plush; felt clothes; 1980s; made by Gabrielle. $125.

Santa Paddington: 12 inches; gold mohair; plastic eyes; not jointed; dressed like Santa Claus; made by Eden, 1982. $85.

Paddington anniversary bears: 9 inches; not jointed; plush; wearing traditional costume or sweater; made for Paddington's thirtieth anniversary; all labels intact; ©1981 Eden Toys. $50-60.

Paddington: 4.5 inches; presented in a small shoping bag; 1987; Eden Toys. $20-25.

Paddingtons: 9 inches; not jointed plush; vinyl raincoat on one; sweater on the other; ©1981 Eden Toys. $45-50.

Paddington: 13 inches; by Gabrielle Designs Ltd., England; mohair with felt clothes; rubber boots; carries a suitcase and comes in a presentation box; limited edition; 1990s. $350.

Aunt Lucy: 13 inches; Paddington's Peruvian aunt; limited edition by Gabrielle Designs Ltd., England; 1990s; detailed clothing; presentation box. $350.

Appliquéd Paddington; Gabrielle Archives.

Advertisement for Paddington showing color separations and final result; 1975; Gabrielle Archives.

Playing cards produced by Film Fair Ltd.; 1978. $45-50.

Paddington cup and saucer: 1-inch cup; made in England; Coalport china; 1978. $125. (*Beth Savino collection*)

Paddington bank: made of plastic; money slot is under the removeable hat; made by M. K. of Finland; circa 1980. $25-30.

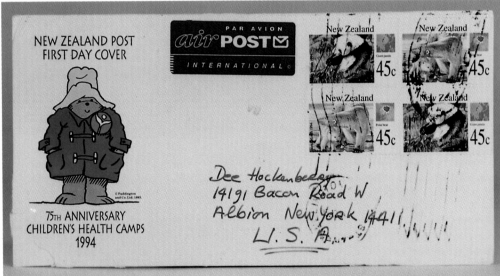

Paddington First Day Cover: issued by the New Zealand Post Office in 1994.

New Zealand stamps: For the anniversary of Children's Health Camps; 1994; Paddington is the Ambassador.

The Busy Bears

The Busy Bears book was written by George W. Gunn and published by I. Austen Co. of Chicago in 1907. According to the advertisement in the G. Sommers catalog of the same year, the tale was bright and catchy, telling a funny bear story in simple words. Of the twelve illustrations, six were in color and six were in black and white.

Following in the wake of publication were several sets of postcards. Given the enormous scope of postcards Printed in the first decade of the twentieth century, it is clear that this form of communication was the method most frequently used. Even though only half of the book illustrations were in color, all of the postcards were. Those numbered from 427 to 432 were Printed several times, thus diverse images often appear with the same caption. For instance Saturday was both mending and baking day. The series numbered 433 through 438 depict school activities with the bears being very busy, and often in trouble.

Busy Bears postcard: "Something Doing." $20.

Book: *The Busy Bears* by George W. Gunn; paperback; hard-to-find book that is the basis for many spin-offs in the form of china and postcards; published by J. I. Austen Co., Chicago; ©1907. $50-150.

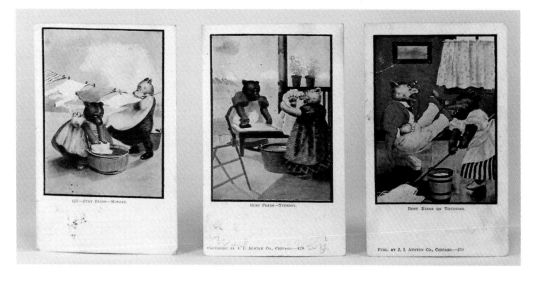

Busy Bears days-of-the-week postcards: Monday washing; Tuesday ironing; Thursday mopping; 1907. $20-40 each.

239

Busy Bears postcard: "On vacation;" No. 438. $30-40.

Busy Bears postcard: "Learning phonetic spelling;" 1907. $20.

Busy Bears postcard: "Off to School;" No. 435. $30-40.

The china examples seem to use school days most often. The pieces were produced in both delicate designs with pink and gold accents and in a heavier, more utilitarian manner. A Christmas theme with pine cones and branches was also popular. None of the samples I have encountered have been marked, but my guess is that they most likely were made in Germany.

Certainly the early 1900s was rife with the production of teddy bears. They were made by multitudes of toy makers; many of whom began and ended their manufacturing process in the space of just a few years. Soft toy bears of all descriptions were advertised and produced ad infinitum, but sadly, to my knowledge, the engaging Busy Bears were not among them.

Busy Bear cocoa pot: 6 inches; fine china; scene of fence painting on the front; flower motif on reverse; note that the handle looks like a ribbon; no marks; 1908. $225-250.

Reverse side of cocoa pot.

Busy Bear creamer: 3 inches; fine china; "Playing Leap Frog;" circa 1908. $75-100.

Busy Bear cups and saucers: 3 inches; fine china; scene from the *Busy Bears Book*; circa 1908. $125 each.

Busy Bear sugar bowl: 4 inches; fine china; "Getting It in the Right Places;" circa 1908. $175-195.

Busy Bear cups: 1.75 inches; two scenes from book; part of a set with pink coloring; circa 1908. $40-45 each.

Busy Bear plate: 6 inches; scene showing "leap frog;" circa 1908. $150-160.

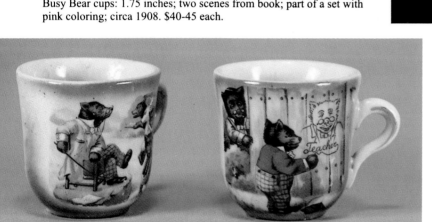

Below left: Busy Bear feeding dish: 7.5 inches; heavy china with deep edges; six scenes of bears in a transfer design; circa 1908. $200-225.
Below: China hot plate: 6.5 inches; scene from *The Busy Bears;* circa 1908. $150-plus.

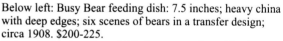

Busy Bear plate: 7.75 inches; china with greens and pine cones around the edge; this is a frequently used scene titled "Getting It in the Right Places;" circa 1908. $175-200.

The Busy Bears teapot: white china touched with pink and showing the familiar "Teacher" illustration. circa 1908. $265-plus.

Busy Bears Christmas dish: 7 inches; china decorated with pine cones around the edge; circa 1908. $165-plus.

Busy Bear book: 4 x 5.5 inches; small format; Ullman's Red Line Series; illustrated by Bernhardt Wall; early 1900s. The only other articles from this book are postcards; this concept causes some confusion among collectors because, although the book and cards are "Busy Bears," it is a completely different series than the the I. Austen book and mementoes. $65-plus.

Days-of-the-week postcards: the "Little Bear" series; illustrated by Wall; ©1905 by the Ullman Mfg. Co. from their *Busy Bear* book, Series 79. $75-85 per set of seven.

Thursday through Sunday postcards by Ullman.

Bibliography

Cockrill, Pauline. *The Ultimate Teddy Bear Book.* London and New York: Dorling Kindersley Inc. 1991

Cohen, Morton N. *Lewis Carroll: A Biography.* New York: Alfred A. Knopf 1995.

Davis, Norma S. *A Lark Ascends—Florence K. Upton Artist and Illustrator.* Metuchen, N. J. and London: The Scarecrow Press Inc. 1992

Green, Roger L. *The Story of Lewis Carroll.* New York: Henry Schuman. 1951

Knox, Rawle ed. *The Work of E. H. Shepard.* New York: Schocken Books. 1980

Linder, Leslie. *The Journal of Beatrix Potter from 1881-1897.* London and New York: Frederic Warne & Co. 1996

Linder, Leslie. *A History of the Writing's of Beatrix Potter.* London and New York: Frederic Warne & Co. 1971

Nicholson, Susan B. *Teddy Bears on Paper.* Dallas: Taylor Publishing Co. 1985

Schoonmaker, Patricia N. *Collector's History of the Teddy Bear.* Cumberland, Maryland: Hobby House Press. 1981

Shepard, Ernest H. *Drawn from Memory.* New York and Philadelphia: J. B. Lippincott Company. 1957

Taylor, Judy. *Beatrix Potter: Artist, Storyteller and Countrywoman.* London and New York: Frederic Warne & Co. 1986

Taylor, Judy. *Beatrix Potter's Letters.* London and New York: Frederic Warne & Co. 1989

Index

Dee Hockenberry lives in a small town in western New York with her husband, Tom, who photographs all her works. They share their home with two cats, a den of teddy bears, and many other toys and related memorabilia. They are the parents of two grown children. Dee is the author of several other collectible books and regularly contributes to three teddy bear magazines. She is recognized internationally as a bear and Steiff animal historian and often lectures on the subject. Along with a partner, she operates a mail-order business selling vintage teddies, animals, and other antique accessories. They may be seen at selected shows in the United States, Europe, and Asia.